The
Power of
Hope

The
Power of
Hope

Overcoming depression,
anxiety, guilt, and stress

Julián Melgosa ►◄ Michelson Borges

IADPA · S P Established 1884

THE POWER OF HOPE
Copyright © 2017 by Review and Herald® Publishing Association.
All rights reserved. Present edition published with permission of the copyright owner.

IADPA

Inter-American Division Publishing Association®
2905 NW 87th Avenue, Doral, Florida 33172, USA
Tel. (305) 599-0037 • mail@iadpa.org • www.iadpa.org

President **Pablo Perla**
Vice president of Editorial Affairs **Francesc X. Gelabert**
Vice president of Production **Daniel Medina**
Vice president of Customer Service **Ana L. Rodríguez**
Vice president of Finance **Saúl Ortiz**

Book Editor
Sabine Honoré

Cover Designer
Elías Peiró Arantegui

Layout Artist
Daniel Medina Goff

Copyright © 2017 of this edition
Inter-American Division Publishing Association®

ISBN: 978-1-61161-828-0

Copyright © 2017 of this edition published with permission of
Inter-American Division Publishing Association® by The Stanborough Press Ltd, Alma Park,
Grantham, NG31 9SL, UK. Tel: 01476 591700

ISBN: 978-1-78665-047-4

Printed in China

Printed September 2017 • Reprinted 2022

Images courtesy of: © iStockphoto.com

Contents

Contents

1

Health:
It's All in Your Head

After a tense day at work, filled with many problems to solve, numerous e-mails to respond to, and telephone calls to return, Paul wanted to get home, eat something, relax on the sofa, and just watch anything on television. However, heavy traffic caused the usual minutes in the car to become hours. It was dark when he finally arrived home. Entering the house, he immediately took off his shoes, threw his briefcase in a corner, said a quick hello to his wife and glanced at his two children who were playing on the carpet. After a warm shower, he put on comfortable clothes and sat at the dinner table.

"Is there anything to eat?" he asked drily.

"Your mother called a while ago. She was complaining that it has been several months since you paid her a visit."

"She knows I don't have time for that. I have more to do than go see her. Bills to pay. Problems to solve. And the new supervisor will not leave me alone. What an impossible woman! I think she's afraid the company will go under. It's really hard to work with her. She's driving me crazy!"

"That's all you talk about lately—problems, bills, and your supervisor. Did you even notice that your children are there in the living room? All afternoon Mark has been asking what time you would get here."

"Are we going to have this discussion again, just like every other day? Complaints and more complaints! They hassle me at work, and then you hassle me at home! Do you think it's easy to support a family with just my salary?"

These last words hit Silvia where it hurt the most. It was not fair. She had left her job for health reasons, and he knew that. While it was a blessing to spend more time with the kids, listening to her husband's mocking reminders day after day was becoming unbearable.

"Our children are growing up and they hardly know their father. And I'm not even going to mention the state of our marriage!"

"Please give me a break! I am tired, I have a headache and no patience to have this conversation right now."

At that moment, Paul's six-year-old daughter handed an envelope to her father.

"Not now, honey! Can't you see that your mother and I are talking?" Paul snapped.

He carelessly stuffed the paper into his pocket, ignoring his little girl, who slunk away with tear-filled eyes.

"Are you that stupid? Can't you see what you are doing to our family?"

"I've had enough! I'm going to bed. I just lost my appetite."

Paul felt that he was losing control of his world. The man who used to be secure and self-assured could no longer manage his own life. Negative thoughts were taking control of his mind. His brain was in turmoil, and bad memories continually made everything worse. His body was in a state of excessive fatigue because of his lack of physical exercise. His stressed-out supervisor constantly demanded reports from him. All he wanted was some rest and sleep—and maybe he could just never wake up.

He lay in bed and when he rolled over on his side, he felt something crinkle in his pocket. Taking out the wrinkled envelope, he opened it and found a note scribbled in crayon. He felt pain in the pit of his stomach as he read the words, "I love you Daddy."

Black Hole

Have you ever felt like Paul, swamped by commitments and unable to deal with so many things at the same time? Have you ever felt like throwing in the towel and running away to some deserted place? Perhaps you are lucky and your days go by calmly, without any mishaps. Right now, millions of people are suffering the effects of anxiety, stress, and depression. These problems have grown increasingly common in our world.

Some time ago, Stephen Hawking, the famous British physicist, made a statement that went viral on social media. His subject was not fantastic theories about different universes. Hawking, who has lived confined to a wheelchair for decades because of a degenerative neurological disease, offered advice to people who suffer from depression. Hawking said, "The message of this lecture is that black holes ain't as black as they were painted. They are not the eternal prisons they were once thought. Things can get out of a black hole both on the outside and possibly to another universe. So if you feel you are in a black hole, don't give up—there's a way out."

Perhaps Hawking's words of encouragement cannot reassure someone like Paul, who is living in a "black hole" of anxiety, depression, and suicidal thoughts. Is there *really* a way out from these problems? *Is* there hope? *Can* a person crawl out of the black holes that this life presents?

The Power of Our Thoughts

The popular saying, "Where there's a will, there's a way," contains a great deal of truth. Every athlete knows that breaking a record is not simply the result of physical preparation, but also comes from cultivating the right thoughts in the mind. Likewise, the things we do, the emotions we feel, and even the illnesses we suffer from have their origin in our thoughts.

The *environment* (people, places, and circumstances), our *personality* (optimist or pessimist, suspicious or trusting, talkative or quiet), and *memories and experiences* are springboards that drive our thoughts. Each person can control their thoughts and direct their will. With the exception of instinctive reactions or repeated actions in our habits, what we do has its origin in our thoughts. Take a look at these three cases:

- Prior to meeting with a real estate agent, Morris had not thought about purchasing property. However, the atmosphere of courtesy, the beautiful photos of the available homes, and the easy payment plan presented encouraged him to consider the possibility of purchasing a home. He went home and thought about the matter. He imagined moving to a larger, more secure residence, with a school in the neighborhood for his children and easy access to public transportation. Within two days, he signed the contract.

- Eloise went out to eat with two old college friends. They had a great time talking about fun memories and about their current situations. Back home, Eloise compared her life to that of her friends. She considered all the details, remembered the past, and came to the conclusion that her friends were happier than she was. Immediately, depression overtook her as she thought about her own life. Her sad mood lasted several days.

- Victoria had a good relationship with almost everyone. Months earlier, she had had an unpleasant argument with her brother, and they weren't speaking to each other. She did not want to make peace with him because she had suffered as a result of his insults. When she remembered the misunderstanding, she became upset and felt nauseated.

In all three cases, there is a clear relationship between thought, behavior, and state of mind. What if Morris, Eloise, and Victoria had changed the course of their thought processes? They all would probably have had a much different reaction.

In any event, we can all control our thoughts. And therefore, with greater or lesser difficulty, we can nurture them, guide them, expand them, decrease them, or reject them.

Many people know what to do when they feel some physical ailment—a cold, a headache, or stomachache. However, few people know what to do when they feel anxious, worried, nervous, upset, or impatient. These are toxic states of mind that should be confronted.

How can you identify negative thoughts? How can you know if they will lead you to undesirable behavior or to a negative state of mind? To avoid improper thoughts, you should adopt a lifestyle that is guided by moral principles and values, such as honesty, responsibility, justice, respect for others, integrity, and truthfulness. The main idea is to cultivate good values and to develop a principled lifestyle that grows gradually. Those who are guided by these principles end up, naturally and spontaneously, nurturing optimistic and edifying thoughts, with the corresponding beneficial results.

In *Mind and Body Health Handbook*, researchers David Sobel and Robert Ornstein demonstrate evidence of the benefits of optimistic thought and the feeling of control over some areas of health:

- *Immunological system.* Human saliva contains chemical substances that protect us from infections. The levels of protection from these substances are more efficient on days when we feel happy and pleased than on the days when we are sad.
- *Cancer.* One group of cancer patients was taught to think in a positive and uplifting manner and to use relaxation techniques. The study showed that the antibodies of these patients became much more active than those found in patients who had not received these instructions.
- *Longevity.* A group of elderly individuals who resided in assisted living centers were given the freedom to make small decisions (the type of evening meal, choosing a movie once a week, etc.). By taking such actions, they proved to be happier and more satisfied. After a year and a half, the mortality index of this group was fifty percent less than that of those who did not have the opportunity to make choices.
- *Post-surgery.* Based on personality data, patients who underwent cardiac surgery were divided into two categories— optimists and pessimists. The optimists recovered more rapidly, suffered fewer complications, and returned to their normal activities sooner than the pessimists.
- *General health.* Research participants were asked to make a list of positive and negative events they might face within the next several years. Two years later, the health condition of all participants was examined. Compared to those with a negative point of view, those who had been optimistic about the future had fewer symptoms of illness.

One way to have an optimistic outlook on life is to reject negative thoughts and substitute them with positive options. Often, without realizing it, our friend Paul was thinking of problems at work, his irritating supervisor, his wife's complaints, and so on. Pessimistic thoughts usually occur automatically and surprise the individual, and they have no logic. Consequently, it is important to identify them and to change this type of thought. Optimistic thinking must be a constant habit of mental activity. It should cover every aspect of life. These are the areas that need to be considered:

- *Positive thought about oneself.* Do not form your self-concept by comparing yourself to television or movie characters or public figures. They present an unrealistic image. Recognize your limitations, and do something to improve yourself. Most importantly, do not forget to emphasize your values and abilities. Reject self-destructive thoughts. Remember the words of Jesus in Luke 21:15: "I will give you words and wisdom that none of your adversaries will be able to resist or contradict."

- *Positive thoughts about the past.* The past cannot be changed. We should accept even the unpleasant events that have taken place. Do not blame the past for today's difficult situations. It is completely useless. Never worry about unpleasant things that happened in the past. Reflect on yesterday's happiness and successes, remember them and enjoy them, and your attitude will become more positive. Consider Paul's counsel in Philippians 3:13, 14: "But one thing I do: Forgetting what is behind and straining toward what is ahead, I press on toward the goal to win the prize for which God has called me heavenward in Christ Jesus."

- *Positive thoughts about the future.* The future can be shaped, so your attitude today affects your success tomorrow. Thinking confidently and having hope will increase your probability of a happier future. And if there is something negative that might happen, plan ahead so that distress will not over-whelm you if it does happen. God promises in Jeremiah 29:11, "I know the plans I have for you, plans to prosper you and not to harm you, plans to give you hope and a future."

- *Positive thoughts in relation to your environment and people.* Put on "tolerance glasses" and observe your surroundings. Although not everything is perfect, you will find some beautiful things and pleasant experiences. Do not judge people but rather respect them and appreciate the good things they do. Seek to understand their problems and help them. This way, your attitude will bring you satisfaction. Follow the advice found in Philippians 2:3: "Do nothing out of selfish ambition or vain conceit, but in humility consider others better than yourselves." Consider also 1 Thessalonians 5:11: "Therefore encourage one another and build each other up."

Sometimes people allow themselves to become controlled by illogical thoughts. These thoughts cause unhappiness and obstacles. Here are some examples:

- "We are surrounded by constant dangers and risks, and it is natural for us to be worried and afraid."
- "People who are needy and unhappy cannot do anything to improve their situation."
- "To be happy and live at peace with myself, I need to feel the approval and love of everyone who knows me."
- "There is always a perfect solution to every problem, and if this solution is not reached, the consequences will be devastating."

These statements are deceitful. Agreeing with them can bring about psychological pain and unhappiness. You should make an effort to identify and analyze your erroneous thoughts. Think carefully so that you can reject them and accept better alternatives.

Control Your Mental Tendencies

Because of our friend Paul's poor quality of life, his thoughts and feelings became increasingly negative. While his physical and emotional issues were the result of a series of factors, much of the unpleasant atmosphere surrounding him had to do with his inner dialog. If his exterior relationships were not going well, his relationship with himself was even worse.

Frequently, individuals have a generalized tendency for positive or negative thoughts. For the most part, this tendency depends on the style of inner dialog that is continual and automatic. Recognizing the type of dialog we carry on with ourselves becomes indispensable so that bad thought habits can be abandoned and positive alternatives can be sought to help resolve these situations. Let's look at Paul's thoughts and think about possible alternatives:

- *Negative self-dialog:* "All of this is horrible." "I can't resolve anything." "My life is worthless." "I'm losing my family."
- *Alternative:* "Things are bad, but they could be worse." "Perhaps, with some effort and patience, I can resolve one thing at a time." "Not everything is perfect, but there are good things in my life." "If I dedicate a little more quality time to my family, I can improve our relationship."

There are people who believe that joy and happiness come about by chance, that these are influenced by circumstances or are a matter of luck. However, most often, joy and happiness are personal choices. Being happy is an option. Some people prefer to be unhappy, but everyone can choose to be an optimist and enjoy a reasonably happy life. Simple choices, if made with determination, can provide much enthusiasm and prevent discouragement. Look at some examples of things you can say: "I have decided to be happy"; "Today, I will be contented and I will not allow discouragement to take ahold of me"; "I am going to look at the bright side of things"; "Even if my supervisor tries to ruin my day, I will not allow myself to get upset."

Being happy and enjoying a life filled with happiness and optimism is a desirable objective. This can be achieved through one's own initiative.

Optimistic thinking is an excellent option for preserving our mental health and reaching our goals. However, we cannot believe that everything is resolved through our thoughts alone. Optimism, although useful, is limited in certain circumstances: the death of a loved one, a natural disaster, or a serious medical diagnosis. In practice, it is impossible to have optimistic thoughts when we are very bitter or in a critical situation. Positive thoughts can even become deceitful and in some cases make us lose sight of certain sad realities.

2

Anxiety:
Excess Future

Some say that anxiety is excess future, depression is excess past, and stress is excess present. Now imagine someone who has an excess of all of these! Laura was such a person.

When she was five years old, Laura's father abandoned her family, pursuing a woman much younger than her mother. Laura's mother had to work hard to maintain the household. Laura spent much of her time at a day care center while her mother wore herself out with two jobs.

Laura frequently heard her mother complain about their lack of money, so Laura began to fear the future. She feared her mother would leave just as her father had. She was afraid of losing her house, her room, her life. She was unable to relax. She continually felt that a disaster was about to happen. Simply put, she was unable to control her negative thought patterns.

Two years filled with an overwhelming routine caused Laura's mother to pay a high price—a serious disease overtook her, and she passed away a few months later. Once again, Laura was abandoned, and her insecurity reached alarming levels.

Adopted by a great-aunt, Laura grew up without the warmth of her mother's love and the protection of her father. She was afraid of everything—especially of the future.

Anxious people suffer from overwhelming apprehension and worry, altering extensively the normality of their life. The most frequent concerns are interpersonal relationships, work, finances, health, and the future in general. Frequently, these persons experience generalized anxiety with no reason.

Anxiety and depression are the most common mental health issues. In large urban centers, one in three persons suffers from anxiety.[1] Unfortunately, the current conditions under which people live favor these problems and bring a great deal of suffering to the afflicted and their families.

How to Prevent and Overcome Anxiety

Frequently, the symptoms of anxiety do not emerge until a stressful situation triggers a crisis. Easily applied prevention activities can deter the emergence of anxiety and can serve to calm the symptoms when they appear:

- *Talk about your problems.* Seek to associate in a close friendship with individuals with whom you can share your experiences. People who are always isolated run a greater risk of developing anxiety. If this is your case, maintain a good relationship with a family member or friend who can fulfill your need of companionship.
- *Practice relaxation.* Tension accompanies all forms of anxiety, and it is essential to know how to relax in a systematic and habitual manner.
- *Use breathing as a means to avoid tension.* It is surprising how some simple breaks and deep breathing exercises (from the abdomen to the thorax) can provide calmness in an anxious or anguishing situation, thereby avoiding complications.

- *Eat properly.* Research shows that avoiding hypoglycemia (low blood sugar) and eating a breakfast that includes protein helps you to maintain the biochemical balance of the body and prevent thoughts that bring about worry. Therefore, eat healthy foods and begin the day with a good breakfast.
- *Find support groups.* These are groups of people with similar problems. In many cities, there are organized therapy groups. In this context, you will learn much through the experience of others, and they can understand your difficulties as well.

Clinical research leads us to the conclusion that the most successful techniques in treating anxiety are based on cognitive-behavioral psychology.[2] Let's take a look at some of them:

- *Thought control.* It has been proven that thought control is effective, especially in matters that trigger anxiety. If, for example, the reason for anxiety is fear of having a fatal disease, identify the thoughts related to this fear (perhaps the illness of a family member) or any idea that triggers a chain of worries that bring about anxiety. At the first sign of this thought approaching, say, "No!" and focus on something else or begin an activity that can distract your mind.
- *Systematic desensitization.* This approach consists of learning relaxation techniques that help identify and confront the source of anxiety. The possibility of success is high, and the procedure is fast. However, it requires the involvement of a psychologist.

These techniques can be efficient but superficial. Many times, the problems relating to anxiety have deep roots, as in the case of Laura and her childhood. In these circumstances, it is necessary to confront the cause of the problem, and not just the symptoms.

Types of Anxiety and Their Symptoms

Generalized anxiety disorder. This type of anxiety can present three or more of the symptoms listed below, on most days within the past six months:

- Feelings of uneasiness or nervousness
- Fatigue
- Difficulty in concentrating
- Irritability
- Muscle tension
- Problems sleeping

Anxiety with panic attack. Four or more of the symptoms listed below can be present with this type of anxiety. They may develop abruptly and reach a peak within ten minutes.

- Heart palpitations or accelerated heartbeat
- Sweating
- Shortness of breath
- Quivers or shaking
- Chills or hot flashes
- Feeling suffocated
- Feelings of panic
- Thoracic pain or discomfort
- Nausea or abdominal discomfort
- Dizziness
- Dry mouth
- Fear of losing control or going crazy
- Fear of dying
- Tingling

Profound Causes of Anxiety

Experience teaches us that personal insecurity and the feeling of failure are profound causes of anxiety. As we will see, Laura aimed to be successful in everything she did to avoid feeling insecure and unsuccessful. It is also common to find a feeling of guilt, as though the individual is responsible for these manifestations. This shows the importance of forgiveness—forgiving ourselves and others.

Personal insecurity and the feeling of failure are related to low self-esteem. Regarding the individual who suffers from a sense of guilt, it is important to examine the past and seek to obtain forgiveness. As we continue Laura's story, you will note that the Holy Spirit was working in her mind (Philippians 4:6, 7) with the purpose of leading her to ask for forgiveness of those she had mistreated at work and to forgive her father who had abandoned her in childhood.

The individual who accepts God as the source of forgiveness receives vast benefits through prayer. This is a reconciling experience that offers a new beginning.

The Turning Point

Little orphan Laura grew up. While in high school, her life made a turnabout. Her great-aunt, who had raised her, did not believe in God and had taught her niece that the universe and life had simply *emerged* billions of years ago. For Laura, human beings were the result of a cosmic accident, and she saw existence as a series of factors that come about through pure chance. Of course, these ideas contributed to her feelings that her life was meaningless.

As a teenager, Laura enjoyed walking on the beach near her home. Often, she strolled until sunset and then would lie down on the sand to watch the stars appear in the sky. She was an intelligent girl and knew a little about astronomy and cosmology. She was aware of the fact that the existence of the universe depended on delicately adjusted laws and very precise parameters. Without them, the entire reality that surrounded her would disintegrate. Observing the starry sky led her mind to the strange conclusion that, if there is a mechanism, like a type of watch, there has to be a watchmaker. But if the watch-maker does not exist, if there is nothing or no one who created everything and who managed everything, what meaning would her life have? What hope would there be for the universe itself?

According to a naturalistic perspective, Laura was sure that there is no future life. She knew that the earth could be destroyed by a solar storm, or that the human race might eliminate itself in a worldwide war. The universe could collapse, crumbling in upon itself, or it could expand indefinitely, consume all energy, and become incapable of maintaining any type of living organism. Was life an illusion? Most people avoid thinking about this, especially because they do not want their life to be based on an illusion. However, they end up doing exactly what they want to avoid; they live based on the illusions of momentary pleasures and passing successes, or the artificial dreams invented by the film industry, electronic games, or various forms of entertainment. Some feel that it is better to ignore cold, hard reality while they live in a consciously illusionary reality.

Laura decided that she would fight to be successful and independent. Abandonment and death would not affect her, because she would not live for anyone else. She would be a good professional. She would earn her money. And then . . . well, then her end would come. Period.

Laura advanced financially and academically, just as she planned. After finishing her undergraduate degree, she obtained her master's degree, landed a great job, moved up the company ladder, and reached a much-coveted position. However, her anxiety did not disappear. There in the back of her mind, a cry for a meaningful life still existed. Without realizing it, Laura ended up transferring all of her anxiety, her stress, and frustrations to her subordinates. She was extremely demanding and, at times, even unjust.

The turning point in Laura's life took place when she met a fellow colleague who seemed different from all her other co-workers. Her colleague was calm, happy, confident, and always had a word of encouragement to offer. Laura was intrigued about the source of hope that seemed to spring from this young woman. Providentially, the two became friends. As they talked, Laura discovered that Christianity is a coherent religion and that the Bible is a trustworthy book, whose historical background is confirmed by dozens and dozens of archeological findings. Laura discovered that the creationist belief that God created the universe and life is not an "old wives' tale." There are consistent philosophical and scientific arguments that seriously challenge the naturalistic, atheistic view, which she had believed up to that point.

She found that numerous Bible texts guarantee that God exists and maintains the life of all of His created beings. It was a very special discovery for Laura to learn that she was not part of a cosmic accident, or that she did not exist by chance. No! She had been planned. Finally her life had a purpose. She was discovering where she had come from, why she existed, and where she was going.

But another discovery was even more liberating for Laura. Reading several books, she realized that such famous personalities as Sigmund Freud and C. S. Lewis had endured problems with their parents in their childhood, and this bad relationship ended up contaminating their view of God. The result was that both of these men became atheists. However, Lewis experienced conversion later in his life which produced a true inner revolution, a change in his heart, thoughts, and feelings. Lewis overcame the past and forgave his father. Freud, according to what is known, never had an experience of this type. He continued as an atheist, although the idea of God always bothered him.

Laura saw herself reflected in these two individuals and in many other people who attribute to God the qualities and defects found in their own father. For Laura, God had abandoned her, just as her father had. But this perception did not correspond to reality. The one who had abandoned her was her flesh-and-blood father. Her heavenly Father had always been by her side.

This is a reality that applies to you also. It does not matter what evil may have been done to you during your childhood— if you suffered abuse by someone close to you or if you were assaulted by someone. God is not that person! God is a loving Father. He only wants what is best for you eternally.

Laura finally discovered that God exists, that He loves her and is by her side. Learning this removed her accumulated burden of anxiety. She would still have to learn many other important things that would adjust her focus and place her on the path to recovery. At that time, however, God's Holy Spirit was planting a seed in her heart. Two ideas would not leave her mind: she needed to forgive her father, and she needed to treat others differently. Divine therapy was having an effect on her life.

Divine Therapy

Anxiety sometimes emerges because of fear of the future. Laura was learning that only God knows the future. This led her to place her faith and trust in the Almighty, who loves and protects those who accept Him. Divine therapy has three aspects:

- *Individual.* The individual needs to influence his or her inner life, taking time to reflect on the fact that life is not summed up in being born, living, and dying. This reflection opens the way for a perspective that goes beyond the here and now. It includes the comprehension of the destiny of the human family and, especially, God's plan for eternal salvation, as explained in the Bible. This helps the individual to acquire a long-term perspective that gives them assurance in the final triumph of good over evil. As a measure for immediate assistance, divine therapy uses the repetition of clear, solid Bible verses. It also includes meditation with a basis in biblical promises, such as, for example, "A thousand may fall at your side, ten thousand at your right hand, but it will not come near you" (Psalm 91:7).

- *Social.* It is not only through worship in community (church service) and through the words of other people that God may intervene. He also does this by the example and the attitude that people demonstrate. The Holy Spirit may use these people to carry out His "therapy." Finally, it's good to mention that God can also use qualified professionals' techniques and strategies to help individuals.

- *Divine.* The divine aspect encompasses the growing intimate relationship between the human being and God through prayer. Prayer consists of talking to God as a friend and counselor: talking about fears, anxieties, doubts and problems, as well as expressing gratitude to the Creator for the good things in our life. Sincere prayer has helped many to grow in faith—which is incompatible with anxiety and uncertainty. Faith, in reality, means trust in God. The more we get to know God through prayer and the study of the Bible, the more we develop this trust, and the more our faith is strengthened.

Assurance Regarding the Future

One of the big doubts Laura harbored as a teenager had to do with the future. The science books she read were useful in certain aspects, but they did not express any hope for the future. In one way or another, the universe would come to an end one day. This does not provide consolation to an anxious person.

Laura evaluated her recent discoveries—that God exists and that He loves her regardless of who she was or what happened to her in the past. This God revealed Himself in a special way in the Holy Bible, and there are many good reasons to believe that this unique book is trustworthy and reliable.

In conversations and studies with her work colleague, Laura discovered that the Bible contains more than 2,500 references to a wonderful future event—the return of Christ. Jesus Himself promised, "Do not let your hearts be troubled. You believe in God; believe also in me. My Father's house has many rooms; if that were not so, would I have told you that I am going there to prepare a place for you? And if I go and prepare a place for you, I will come back and take you to be with me that you also may be where I am" (John 14:1–3).

At the time Jesus returned to heaven—after He had spent three decades on Earth, died on the cross and was resurrected—two angels came to console His disciples with these words: " 'Men of Galilee,' they said, 'why do you stand here looking into the sky? This same Jesus, who has been taken from you into heaven, will come back in the same way you have seen him go into heaven' " (Acts 1:11). How? In what manner? Personally, visibly, among the clouds and surrounded by angels. It will be the most spectacular event in history!

Revelation 1:7 states that every eye will see Jesus—believers and unbelievers alike. Laura understood it would not be intelligent on her part to ignore the various prophecies related to Jesus's return that have already been fulfilled. She was convinced of the promises that He will return. Jesus never lied, and He would not play around with such a serious matter that has nurtured the faith and hope of innumerable Christians throughout history.

Actually, what the Bible teaches is "to live self-controlled, upright and godly lives in this present age, while we wait for the blessed hope—the appearing of the glory of our great God and Savior, Jesus Christ" (Titus 2:12, 13).

Another subject where Laura found relief was the question of what is referred to as "eternal hell." In his book, *Is Your Soul Immortal?* Robert Leo Odom writes, "Suppose, for example, that the judge of your county should sentence a man convicted of murder to be tortured continuously day and night with scalding water and red-hot irons so as to keep him constantly suffering the most excruciating pain. What would the news media have to say about that? What would be the reaction of people in general to a punishment of that sort? Does it make sense to say that our Creator, who is a God of justice and love, could be a monster of cruelty worse than that?"[3]

The idea of eternal torment goes against the just and loving character of God. The Bible affirms that the unjust will be consumed (Revelation 20:8, 9), and they will become ashes (Malachi 4:1–3) by their own choice, as a result of their rebellion. But how should the expression "eternal fire" be understood? Odom explains: "It is not the suffering that is said to be eternal, but the fire which God employed to destroy them is eternal in its effect. . . . By the word 'unquenchable' [Luke 3:17] he means fire that no man can extinguish or put out"[4] (see also 2 Peter 3:7, 10). A good example of punishment by eternal fire is what took place at Sodom and Gomorrah (Jude 7). These cities are not still burning today. They were extinguished.

Laura was very pleased to understand this, because it had been another barrier between her and the God she hadn't known before. When she thought about the myth of eternal hellfire, in her mind she could not see a loving Father. It was contradictory and illogical. But the Bible has nothing to do with this myth. The future presented for the redeemed is a place and a time where there will be no more "death or mourning or crying or pain" (Revelation 21:4).

Obviously, for Laura to overcome anxiety, professional support proved to be beneficial for her. However, her recently acquired knowledge of the God of the Bible and hope in the return of Jesus was decisive in turning her toward the peace that began to fill her life. Now she was no longer afraid of the future, because she knew that God was already there, waiting for her with open arms—a good Father who never abandons His children.

Biblical Solutions to Anxiety

We can find wonderful remedies in verses such as these:

- "The Lord himself goes before you and will be with you; he will never leave you nor forsake you. Do not be afraid; do not be discouraged" (Deuteronomy 31:8).
- "Have I not commanded you? Be strong and courageous. Do not be afraid; do not be discouraged, for the Lord your God will be with you wherever you go" (Joshua 1:9).
- "When anxiety was great within me, your consolation brought me joy" (Psalm 94:19).
- "So do not fear, for I am with you; do not be dismayed, for I am your God. I will strengthen you and help you; I will uphold you with my righteous right hand" (Isaiah 41:10).
- "Do not be anxious about anything, but in every situation, by prayer and petition, with thanksgiving, present your requests to God" (Philippians 4:6).
- "Therefore I tell you, do not worry about your life, what you will eat or drink; or about your body, what you will wear. Is not life more than food, and the body more than clothes? Look at the birds of the air; they do not sow or reap or store away in barns; and yet your heavenly Father feeds them. Are you not much more valuable than they?" (Matthew 6:25, 26).

---

1. A. J. Baxter et al., "Global Prevalence of Anxiety Disorders: A Systematic Review and Meta-regression," *Psychological Medicine* 43, no. 5 (May 2013): pp. 897–910, doi:10.1017/S003329171200147X.

2. F. Hohagen et al., "Combination of Behavior Therapy With Fluvoxamine in Comparison With Behavior Therapy and Placebo: Results of a Multicentre Study," *The British Journal of Psychiatry* 173, Sppl. 35 (August 1998): pp. 71–78;

K. O'Connor et al., "Cognitive-Behaviour Therapy and Medication in the Treatment of Obsessive-Compulsive Disorder: A Controlled Study," *The Canadian Journal of Psychiatry* 44, no. 1 (1999): pp. 64–71; K. Salaberria and E. Echeburúa, "Long-term Outcome of Cognitive Therapy's Contribution to Self-exposure *In Vivo* to the Treatment of Generalized Social Phobia," *Behavior Modification* 22, no. 3 (July 1998): pp. 262–284, doi:10.1177/01454455980223003; A. Stravynski and D. Greenberg, "The Treatment of Social Phobia: A Critical Assessment," *Acta Psychiatrica Scandinavica* 98, no. 3 (September 1998): pp. 171–181.

3. Robert Leo Odom, *Is Your Soul Immortal?* (Hagerstown, Maryland: Review and Herald®, 1989), p. 63.

4. Ibid., p. 69.

3

Depression:
Excess Past

In 2009, crowds were enchanted with the scenes of the idyllic world designed by the screenwriter and film director James Cameron, in his film *Avatar*. What no one could have foreseen is that many people would end up suffering from "post-*Avatar* depression." Websites were created where fans shared their regrets about not living on Pandora, a planet they considered far superior to Earth.

Some comments caused great concern, such as one from a young man named Mike: "Ever since I went to see *Avatar* I have been depressed. Watching the wonderful world of Pandora and all of the Na'vi made me want to be one of them. I cannot stop thinking about all the things that happened in the film and all the tears and shivers I got from it. I even contemplate suicide thinking that if I do it, I will be rebirthed in a world similar to Pandora, and everything is going to be the same as in *Avatar*."

This is a vivid example of the influential power of the media. People want to escape reality and flee to dream worlds, regardless of whether they are real or virtual. And it is not just the *Avatar* fans. There are people who do not go one week (or even one day) without immersing themselves in some film. Others anxiously await the next broadcast of their favorite TV program or soap opera. Some people drop everything so they will not miss the game of their beloved sports team. And what can be said about the hours upon hours spent playing video games or surfing the Internet? They attempt to fill the emptiness of their soul with nourishment that lacks nutrients and has been refined in the studios of those who think only about the money they are going to earn by way of those who are trapped by their addictive productions. This depression, however, is symptomatic. It demonstrates that people are missing something, but they have no idea what it is.

Another behavior that can lead to depression and even generate suicidal thoughts is casual sex. A study carried out by the University of California with 3,900 students showed that people who are involved in sex outside of marriage were more plagued with problems of depression and anxiety than those who are not. The researchers believe that this stress is the result of regret.

The causes of depression vary a great deal. At times they are difficult to identify. This is not a perfect world, and the further we get from the ideal of the One who created the world, the higher the price people pay for this disparity.

The fact is that only those who have faced or now face a depressive state are able to understand what it means to, for example, sleep more than twelve hours at a time, without any desire to wake up; to cry excessively with no apparent reason; to feel unable to enjoy what they like the most; to feel incapable and inept; to have unpleasant thoughts and lose the will to live; to nurture a sense of guilt concerning unimportant things, as well as the feeling of failure; to live locked inside oneself, in the midst of shadows that insist on hovering above one's head. In fact, this is not living but only existing, and eventually it reaches the point when thoughts turn suicidal.

Depression is a great modern disorder in relation to mental health. It is the disease that predominates in consultations in psychiatric and psychology clinics. It is ever-increasing: estimates show that depression will occupy second place among the causes of diseases and incapacity in the world by the year 2020, only remaining behind cardiovascular diseases.

In its corresponding variations, depression affects everyone: children, teenagers, young adults, middle-aged adults, and the elderly; men and women; people from all classes—rich and poor. The World Health Organization (WHO) calculates that more than one hundred million people are depressed in the world.

Suffering a great disappointment, having excessive worry, or feeling stressed does not necessarily mean one has depression. However, these emotional alterations can be the beginning of depression, and it is necessary to be attentive so these feelings do not continue too long.

The symptoms of depression are varied, and a diagnosis is not confirmed until several of them appear in a regular manner during a period of two weeks, and at least one of the symptoms is sadness or the loss of interest or pleasure in normal activities. However, the emergence of only one symptom should serve as a warning to take measures before the solution becomes more difficult.

How to Prevent Depression

- *Seek sufficient social support.* Depression is not frequent in circles where there are strong relationship ties, whether they are through marriage, family, work, or friendships. Therefore, it is important to be part of a happy family, or to be surrounded by good friends, or to have a good work environment, or all three, because these relationships are safeguards against depression. However, how can all of this be accomplished? This is what we will see throughout this book.

- *Keep up an active life.* It is surprising how a weakened state of mind can rapidly change when you occupy yourself with some kind of activity. To avoid depression, take action and find something to do. Perhaps it might be difficult to pay a visit to a friend or talk with a neighbor, but this feeling occurs only in the beginning. Once the activity has begun, you will notice that it is easier to continue. Occupy yourself with tasks that bring you satisfaction and that are productive and uplifting: straighten up your house, fix something, or talk with someone special on the phone. If you are physically able to, practice sports or aerobic physical exercise. Fatigue in this case is the source of health and good humor.

- *Think correctly.* As people concentrate on the negative aspect of something or on the positive side of things, they have a greater or lesser tendency toward depression. Positive thinking is a habit and should be cultivated to avoid a negative outlook on life.

- *Look at the past with caution.* The past can be a source of depression or emotional well-being. Instead of thinking of past adversities, cheer yourself up with thoughts of good times and joyful events. If you have some trauma from the past (abuse, upheaval, etc.), seek out a psychologist or psychiatrist who can help you to identify a way to overcome what has happened.

"Ghosts" from the Past

Depression can also be considered "excess of the past." This was the exact problem Carlos was facing. Carlos was considered a strong and energetic man, so much so that his friends called him Big Carlos. But the years of an out-of-control lifestyle filled with partying, drinking, and casual love relationships had taken their toll. At age seventy, Big Carlos was a shadow of the man he had been in the past. He spent the greater part of his time seated in a wheelchair, silent and mulling over thoughts, while time slowly crept by in the nursing home. His large body was arched constantly under an apparent weight—the weight of memories.

Carlos had been diagnosed with terminal cancer. In past years, he had suffered from a profound depression. He was a man of few words, and he never received visits from relatives. It seemed that everyone had abandoned him when the vigor of his life had gone out of him.

The truth is, in the arms of women and in mugs of beer, Carlos had sought to quiet the voice of his conscience. He never wanted to give in and admit that only once in his life had he experienced something that seemed like true happiness. The more he attempted to deny it, the more his thoughts returned to that one woman, his first girlfriend and ex-wife, whom he did not appreciate at the time. Now she was no longer there to hear his complaints and his talk about living life far away from the "burdens" of a family, the worries of children, and the love of just one woman. How wrong he had been! How had he been able to believe such a lie as though it had been truth?

Carlos did not realize that, even if God decided not to heal him, He could forgive him of all his sins and give him eternal salvation. Wasn't this what Jesus had guaranteed to the thief crucified beside Him? "'Jesus, remember me when you come into your kingdom,' the thief implored. Jesus responded, 'You will be with me in paradise'" (Luke 23:42, 43).[1]

Unfortunately, Carlos did not know this. And had he had the strength and the chance, he would have taken his own life to hasten his inevitable end.

35

Suicide

According to the World Health Organization (WHO), suicide takes more than 800,000 lives per year. Every three seconds, a person attempts to take their own life. This phenomenon ends in the death of one person every forty seconds. In the United States, it is estimated that 121 people take their life every single day. The most common reason for these cases of suicide is untreated depression.

Aiming to clarify this topic in a worldwide awareness campaign,[2] WHO has published a list of myths and facts about suicide. The campaign, for example, refers to the myth that "people who talk about suicide have no intention of committing suicide." The reality is that people who talk about suicide are likely seeking help, since they frequently suffer from anxiety, depression, and lack of hope.

Another myth is that the majority of suicides take place without any warning. The truth is that the majority of suicidal individuals give warnings or signs. Therefore, it is important to know these symptoms and to be able to identify them in the behavior of those around us.

Another classic mistake regarding suicide is thinking that only people with mental problems commit suicide. In reality, many people who have mental problems do not manifest suicidal behavior. On the other hand, not all people who take their own life have mental disorders.

According to the campaign, talking openly about suicide does not encourage it. On the contrary, talking can help the person with suicidal tendencies to analyze other options and give them time to rethink the decision to end their life. People who consider taking their own life almost always have an altered perception of reality. Therefore, it is very important to treat this distortion of reality in order to prevent suicide.

Two other myths are that people who threaten to kill themselves just want attention, and that when someone demonstrates signs of improvement or survives a suicide attempt, the individual is out of danger. The days following a suicide attempt require careful attention, since the survivor will be especially fragile.

Finally, there are those who think that the media should not deal with the topic of suicide, because they think this will encourage suicides. Actually, according to WHO, the media *should* deal with this public health matter and approach the topic appropriately. Everyone needs to be informed regarding suicide and should know where to seek help. Additionally, it is essential to critically analyze the content of media. Unfortunately, there are songs, TV programs, movies, and even electronic games that may incite suicide. Preteens and teenagers should receive special attention and education about suicide.

According to WHO, it is possible to prevent suicide in ninety percent of cases. There are organizations prepared to offer assistance. For example, in the United States the National Suicide Prevention Lifeline (800-273-TALK or 800-273-8255) offers twenty-four-hour toll-free suicide prevention service, along with a website (suicidepreventionlifeline.org); emergency help can be accessed by dialing 911; and Crisis Text Line (crisistextline.org) is a nationwide 24/7 text-message hotline that provides crisis intervention when someone texts HELLO to 741741. Telephone numbers for suicide hotlines for a variety of situations can also be found at www.suicide.org.

How to Overcome Depression

Treatment for depression is carried out in two forms—pharmacology and psychotherapy. In the majority of the cases, initial pharmacological treatment is prescribed by a family doctor or psychiatrist. At the same time, a psychological intervention plan is followed, which prepares the individual to get relief from the depression and avoid its return.

- *Pharmaceutical products.* In some cases, antidepressants can bring relief from the psychological pain and minimize the tendency toward suicide that frequently accompanies the depressed individual. Antidepressants work on the brain's chemistry with the objective of balancing the activity of the neurotransmitters in the brain. In many cases, this alleviates the symptoms and can strengthen the effects of psychotherapy. At times, it is necessary to submit the patient to various types of medications until the best one is found. A wait of several weeks is necessary to see the results—which is the reason some patients abandon the medication without medical supervision and therefore worsen the situation. Additionally, the antidepressant medications can produce side effects of varied intensity.

Psychotropic medication is like a regulator on a watch that is running too fast or too slow. The big problem is that it only works at the speed at which the watch functions. For this reason, in spite of bringing some pleasure, antidepressant medication can become inefficient and even dangerous if used in an inappropriate manner.

- *Daily routine.* Planning a program of activities is one of the most common strategies used by psychologists. It is a schedule that the patient will fulfill over several weeks. The psychologist plans the schedule with the help of the patient's family. As it is put into practice, the sick individual occupies the necessary time and acquires new behavior patterns to avoid a relapse. A good schedule of activities should take into consideration the following principles:

➤ Choose the most pleasant activities and avoid, especially in the beginning, those that are considered excessively difficult.

➤ Seek activities that have a social component. It is better to have a get-together with friends than to watch a movie alone.

➤ If possible, do not interrupt normal work, but continue working or studying, although reducing the number of hours and the intensity.

➤ In the majority of cases, manual work is advised— carpentry, sewing, or gardening.

➤ Include physical exercise whenever the patient's health allows. The chemical and hormonal balance produced by pharmaceutical medications can also be obtained or complemented with sports and physical activity.

➤ The schedule of planned activities should be as detailed as possible (for example: an activity from 8:00 to 8:30 a.m., then another from 8:30 to 9:00 a.m., and so on).

• *Way of thinking.* In the treatment of depression, the individual must intentionally focus on their thought patterns. Those who suffer from depression have the tendency to:

➤ Have unrealistic objectives and expectations. For example, a man becomes depressed because he thinks that he has not been successful in business, even though his business is going well.

➤ Point out personal failures and minimize their achievements. A young woman won a literary contest. When her friends congratulated her, she insisted on saying that few people had entered the contest—or that they gave her the award out of pity.

➤ Compare themselves to others and feel they are inferior. A woman attends a high school reunion and returns home depressed because she considers the achievements of her former classmates superior to hers.

For a successful treatment, thought restructuring should be included, because depression strengthens the negative thoughts of the individual about their environment and toward the future. The person should avoid all thoughts of inferiority and self-pity. Instead, they should think that a great part of their success depends on what they plan to do, and count their personal qualities and capabilities to be of great value.

In an assessment of the environment, the person should not concentrate on imperfections or dangers. Rather, they should focus on the beautiful things in life and pleasant memories. Certainly, there are many good things to think about. And if there are negative things going on, the person should do something to withstand them instead of feeling self-pity.

- *Family support.* Professional treatment progresses considerably better if the family offers support to the depressed individual. It is of vital importance, when a spouse, child, or some other family member suffers from depression, that the problem is faced seriously. In addition, follow this guidance:
  ➤ Listen with attention and sympathy, because this alone produces a therapeutic effect.
  ➤ Never censure the person, but treat them calmly and naturally.
  ➤ Help your family member to keep occupied—plan outings, entertainment, small tasks, etc.
  ➤ Encourage the individual and nurture hope that he or she will come out of the depressed state with dignity.
  ➤ Support their medical treatment by reminding the patient of the importance of taking their medication. Also, avoid transmitting doubts such as, "What are these pills

for?" or "Why do you need to go to a psychiatrist? You are not crazy!" If you are in doubt about the treatment, speak with the doctor and not the patient.

➤ Expect difficulties, especially if the individual's condition becomes worse and he or she begins to say that life is not worth living and that they wish to die.

➤ Monitor the individual so that he or she eats adequately and does not use alcohol.

- *Do something for others.* Acts of service help the depressed individual to understand that he or she can offer assistance to others. This offers fresh encouragement and is therapeutic. The person may try caring for a friend's child, go shopping for an elderly individual, visit someone who is hospitalized, or do small volunteer jobs. Acting in this manner, the individual will forget his or her own suffering and notice there are people who have greater necessities than their own. Helping other people is a way to help yourself.

- *Look to the future with hope.* If you are feeling the symptoms of depression, you need to understand that the future is not at the mercy of circumstances and you are an important part of tomorrow. Flee from all feelings of desperation and incapability.

- *Explain failures with reality.* Be aware of your strengths and weaknesses. Analyze situations in a well-balanced manner. For example, if you were not successful at getting a particular job, do not think of yourself as useless. Instead, consider whether it was a difficult job to obtain or if there were a large number of candidates. The next time, try to better prepare yourself for the position you want.

- *Assume control of future events.* Much of what you experience can be shaped by choices. For example, if the origin of your problems is family related, do not think that there is no longer a solution for the relationships. You can do something to improve your way of communicating. There are real ways to improve your future.

- *Divine therapy.* Trusting that God is willing to help, protect, and favor those who seek Him is the first step to benefiting from spirituality. This conviction produces a relationship that inspires inner peace. It is the same feeling as that of a little boy who walks along a rocky path holding his father's hand; he is not afraid because he feels safe because of his father's strong hand. In the same way, along the path of life, the individual who trusts in God knows that there are risks of all types, but a faith in the Creator allows the individual to look to the future with peace of mind because he or she is certain that their heavenly Father will be there to protect them.

Specific spiritual help is available through prayer to God, like talking to a friend with whom one shares concerns; and reading the Bible with its stories and messages that bring inner peace. Select several short texts and memorize them so that you can recall them in times of crisis. Finally, seek to associate with people who share these same ideas. This association can serve as a bridge of support to improve your trust in God.

In a study carried out in the city of San Francisco after the earthquake that struck the city in 1989, it became clear that the people who used a system of social support to fight against the psychological aftereffects of the earthquake demonstrated low levels of depression and anxiety. However, those who had isolated themselves reached high levels of depression. This was verified not only during the days following the earthquake but also seven weeks after the catastrophe.

If you are accustomed to isolating yourself and thinking too much about your anguish, change your attitude and your approach, or you will rapidly fall into depression. It is recommended that you have a friend or confidante with whom you can share your anxieties.

Antidepressants: Limitations and Problems

Antidepressant medications can bring some temporary relief to the very unpleasant symptoms of depression. However, they do not cure the disease. The elimination of the agents that cause the stress, along with changes of attitude and behavior through the help of psychotherapy, is what can really contribute to the cure.

The patient who uses antidepressant medication will not feel improvement for at least two or three weeks after beginning the treatment. Additionally, the following side effects are sometimes observed: problems with sexual performance; cardiovascular alterations; sleepiness (or insomnia); blurred vision; nervousness; constipation; weight gain (or loss); and dry mouth.

The physician Marcia Angell, who was the editorial director for the *New England Journal of Medicine*, points out that a review of studies on antidepressants reached the conclusion that the major medications prescribed for this purpose have little more than a placebo effect.[3]

Considering these findings, a change of lifestyle is the best medicine for overcoming depression and the majority of chronic diseases.

Do Not Blame the Past

Past experiences have an important effect on thought patterns, but they do not have to define one's mental health. It is necessary to accept the past, which cannot be changed, and avoid the passivity of doing nothing to improve the present and the future. Therefore, never let yourself say, "My past has determined who I am," or "I am like this because I had a complicated childhood," or "I have this problem because my parents did not know how to bring me up." This attitude compromises the process of rehabilitation and blocks many sources of assistance and support.

Even though depression usually requires medical and psychological intervention, self-help strategies also provide a significant benefit to treatment and prevention. Here are some tips:

- *Count on a friend or a confidante.* Find someone who appreciates you and understands you, so you can talk naturally. Meditating alone about one's problems is the worst activity for the depressed individual.

- *Keep yourself busy.* Go out in the fresh air and practice some type of sport; or, if you prefer, stay home doing some type of manual activity. Activities keep you busy and will not allow your mind to become occupied with thoughts that reinforce depression.

- *Eliminate alcohol completely.* It is a habit of some to try and drown their sadness in alcohol. However, do not be deceived. This substance may relieve the symptoms for a few hours, but the destruction it causes to physical and mental health is quite serious. It is important to remember that alcohol unleashes a snowball-type response. Alcohol depresses the activity of the cerebral neurons, those that accompany the circuits responsible for self-control, as well as those that can help an individual to have a positive attitude. The euphoria from alcohol is fleeting, and it is followed by feelings of inadequacy, guilt, and uselessness.

- *Maintain a healthy diet.* Eat vegetables, fresh fruit, cereals, and legumes. If you have not yet developed the habit of eating in this manner, it will be difficult at first. However, after a while, you will grow accustomed to it.

- *Protect yourself from insomnia.* Exercise, eat a light evening meal, and avoid thoughts that cause worry. If sometimes you have difficulty sleeping, do not become impatient. Make yourself comfortable on a sofa and read a book or listen to the radio until you are able to sleep.
- *Think about good things.* Concentrate on things that bring you satisfaction, and be certain that all periods of adversity will come to an end. Additionally, we have many things to be grateful for. We should often revisit the reasons for our gratitude.
- *Assume a hopeful attitude.* Hope is a human necessity. Without it, doubt and fear and anxiety emerge. People who have hope in the future and a relationship with our loving God are powerfully protected against depression.

Carlos's problem, mentioned at the beginning of this chapter, was that he refused to talk about his fears and feelings, and the certain nearness of death worsened his depressive state. A heavy anchor seemed to be holding him to the past, and there was a dark, unknown road ahead of him, filling him with fear and uncertainty.

Confronting Death

Like the fans of *Avatar*, Carlos sadly discovered that Pandora does not exist. He wasted all of his opportunities to live a happy life. His wife had left many years ago, and his daughter did not want to see him under any circumstances. The approaching end to his existence was certain, and he did not have any comfort through faith to receive divine forgiveness and the hope of eternal life with Christ.

If only Carlos had known what the Bible says about life after death! Then he could rest upon this hope. When the Bible describes the death of the saved, it is always through the lens of hope.

To understand what takes place at death, it is necessary to know *how* human beings were created. In Genesis 2:7, it is written: "And the Lord God formed man of the dust of the ground, and breathed into his nostrils the breath of life; and man became a living soul" (KJV).

It is important to note that the text states that we *are* a living soul and not that we *have* a soul. The word *soul* in the original Hebrew is *nephesh*, which means "to be living." Therefore, dust of the earth + breath of life = living soul ("to be living"). Genesis 3:19 states that after death, the human being returns to the dust. The equation looks like this: dust of the earth - breath of life = the soul no longer exists (dust returns to dust; breath returns to God). When a human being dies, the breath (spirit) returns to God, the dust returns to the earth, and the living soul no longer exists; in other words, it dies. The apostle Paul is very clear in affirming that only God is immortal (1 Timothy 6:15, 16).

Many people think it is possible to maintain contact with the dead. However, we learn in the Bible that the dead remain in a state of unconsciousness, incapable of communicating with the living. This is very clear in Bible texts such as Ecclesiastes 9:5, 6 and Psalm 146:4, among others. Therefore, the spirits that appear here and there in the Bible are actually evil angels or demons who pose as people who have died (Revelation 16:14; 2 Corinthians 11:14).

In the story of Lazarus's death and resurrection (John 11:1–44), Jesus calls death a *sleep*, reaffirming the concept of unconsciousness. When He calls Lazarus from the grave, in a demonstration that He has the power to resurrect anyone from the dead, Jesus says nothing about His friend Lazarus regarding heaven, hell, or even "tunnels of light." Lazarus was dead, in an unconscious sleep of rest. Furthermore, it would be a tremendous injustice on the part of Christ to call His friend back to this sad life, subject to disease and death, if he had been enjoying eternal life in Paradise.

To die is to sleep unconsciously, awaiting the resurrection. The Bible says nothing of going to hell immediately, going to heaven immediately, or any cycle of reincarnation. Hebrews 9:27, 28 is a very clear text: "Just as people are destined to die once, and after that to face judgment, so Christ was sacrificed once to take away the sins of many; and he will appear a second time, not to bear sin, but to bring salvation to those who are waiting for him."

Where and how did the lie about the immortal soul begin? To obtain this answer, we have to return to the book of origins, to Genesis 2:16, 17 and 3:4. It states that the Creator made it very clear to Adam and Eve that the consequence of sin (separating themselves from the Source of life) is death. Satan, the enemy of God, openly contradicted the divine Word and guaranteed Eve that she would not die. Upon listening to the voice of evil, Eve sinned, and then Adam sinned. We all inherited the consequences of this sad choice of our first parents.

Our loving Creator did not abandon us in this world of sin. The Bible is filled with promises related to the resurrection and the gift of eternal life to all who accept the salvation offered by the Lord. Texts such as 1 Thessalonians 4:16 and 1 Corinthians 15:51 make it very clear that the dead in Christ will be resurrected when Jesus returns. Additionally, another thing that the Bible makes very clear is that no one will be "left behind." All who accept Jesus's gift of salvation, even if they die, will be resurrected when Jesus comes a second time, according to His own promise (John 14:1–3). Those who have scorned salvation will remain dead for one thousand years, awaiting the close of God's judgment, as explained in Revelation 20.

There will be two distinct resurrections (John 5:28, 29), separated by an interval of one thousand years. The determining factor for us to participate in the first resurrection is our relationship with Jesus today. Only through Him is there eternal life

(1 John 5:12; John 3:16). And only as we are connected to Him, like the branches on a tree (John 15:1–9), can we also live eternally in a world where peace and love reign (Revelation 21:4).

Be assured that "the Lord is close to the brokenhearted and saves those who are crushed in spirit" (Psalm 34:18). He is willing to forgive our sins and offer us eternal life. Knowing this can help us to face the sadness, hurts, and deceptions in our life with much greater strength and courage.

---

1. Some Bible translations state the text thus: "Truly I tell you, today you will be with me in paradise." In fact, Jesus could not have said to the saved thief that he would be in Paradise at the moment of his death because Jesus Himself had not risen to heaven after the crucifixion (see John 20:17). The thief knew that his resurrection would take place when Jesus came into His kingdom at His second coming (John 14:1–3; 1 Thessalonians 4:16). What causes confusion about Luke 23:43 is the placement of the comma before the word *today*. In Greek this type of punctuation does not exist, and therefore the comma would be correctly placed after the word *today*, indicating that Jesus was affirming the salvation of the thief at that moment in time.

2. Alexandra Fleischmann et al., eds., *Preventing Suicide: A Global Imperative* (Geneva: World Health Organization, 2014).

3. "Antidepressivos Trazem Mais Prejuízos do que Benefícios" ["Anti- depressants Bring More Harm Than Good"], *O Globo*, oglobo.globo.com/sociedade/saude/antidepressivos-trazem-mais-prejuizos-do-que-beneficios-2896469, last updated November 3, 2011.

4

Stress:
Excess Present

Do you remember Paul from chapter 1 of this book? He was the husband who would arrive home upset with his supervisor and never had time for his wife and kids. His big problem is stress. Actually, this is an increasingly common problem in the lives of millions of people.

Stress is part of our daily life. Time and work pressures, problems in relationships, noise, pollution, finances, and insecurity are only a few causes of stress.

The consequences of stress affect our body, mind, and emotions. Stress should be monitored, because its effects can cause damage and can even lead to fatality. On the other hand, in the right quantity, stress is a good source of motivation. Stress mechanisms release energy so the individual can face almost any situation. Some even classify it like this: *stress*—physiological condition, necessary and useful in life and survival; *distress*—condition of imbalance, prejudicial to health.

Eveline, a tailor, provides an example. She knows that Friday is the day she delivers her sewing orders, and she works untiringly on Thursday. In fact, on Thursday she produces more than on Tuesday and Wednesday together. She concentrates better and works more quickly and with greater precision—she even forgets to eat! On Fridays, she delivers the clothing on time and relaxes with satisfaction. Stress was useful on this occasion. But she cannot abuse this energy constantly. The worst effects of stress emerge when situations like this one become extended or exaggerated. This is the case for Paul, who had already surpassed his defense barrier. When an individual oversteps the barrier of adequate stress, the body consequently lowers the resistance of the immunological system that protects us against infections. We then become more prone to acquiring all types of diseases, including colds. Now imagine stress aligned with depression. What could this pair be capable of doing? Could this have been the trigger for Carlos's cancer?

Physical and Psychological Effects of Stress

Stress has an influence on various diseases, and the state of imbalance caused by bad stress weakens the mind and the body to face these situations. Thoughts, emotions, and behavior also feel the effects of excessive stress:

- *Thought:* difficulty thinking correctly, faulty memory, lack of concentration, mistaken concepts, etc.
- *Emotions:* constant tension, fear of contracting some type of disease, impatience and irritability, insecurity, etc.
- *Behavior:* a decline in verbal flow, a risk of the use of dangerous substances, habitual absence from school and from work, difficulty sleeping, relationship problems, etc.

Permanent Stress: Great Danger

Our friend Paul had not yet developed a physical disease; however, he was on the path toward doing so. He urgently needed to change his lifestyle, or he and his family would pay a high price. When work production is maintained at the cost of high stress and great tension, efficiency is lost. And when the duration of high stress is prolonged, the risk for serious disorders in the body and mind increases.

How to Prevent Stress

A wise use of time prevents stress, and we need to know how to manage it. Time is one of the assets that everyone receives in the same measure, and how we feel depends on how we spend it. How can a person use time in a balanced manner?

- *Be realistic.* Perhaps you recognize the saying, "Don't bite off more than you can chew." It advises us against trying to do too many things at once. We have a fundamental need to set goals that can be carried out in the time available.

- *Establish priorities.* Knowing your priorities makes it easier to concentrate on the tasks that are most important. This has a lot to do with your values and your beliefs. What position does money occupy in your life? What is the importance of your work? How do you consider your family relationships? Do you regard helping other people as worthwhile? Do you demonstrate religious values in your life? Depending on your answers, you will designate adequate time for each aspect of your life.

- *Diversify your tasks.* Focusing time and energy on one activity for too long can cause it to become boring—or an obsession. Work is important for you to receive an income and personal satisfaction. A couple or family relationship is also an ingredient of good balance. Leisure offers much satisfaction and should be a complement to regular work; therefore, it does good to alternate physical work with calm leisure activities or sedentary work with active leisure pursuits.

- *Be organized.* Prepare a list of things you need to do during the day and the week. Focus on them, and do not get distracted by other things that take your attention from your desired objectives. If you feel extreme pressure, decrease some of the activities. If you think that the tasks are too few, experiment by adding something more.

- *Live a simple life.* Leisure activities that absorb a great deal of time, such as expensive vacations and extravagant sports, can become causes of stress in themselves. These examples involve not only large amounts of money but also the use of time and energy for them to be implemented. Try simple activities such as an outing in the open air or reading a good book. Learn to be happy with simple things that provide true joy.

How to Overcome Stress

The treatment for stress has to be complete and holistic. It should encompass all social aspects of one's life (work, family, friends, etc.). In periods of a stress crisis, choose the amount of work that can reasonably be carried out, and do not be concerned about anything else. Give attention to your relationships, forget about yourself, seek to be pleasant, and offer your friendship to others. Help someone, be friendly, and make a contribution to humanity. The reaction of others will help you.

Overcoming stress involves all the dimensions of existence: physical, mental, and spiritual. Consider the following guidance:

- *Thought plan.* The most efficient therapy in stress cases is called cognitive psychotherapy, which consists of teaching an individual to control his or her thoughts instead of allowing the thoughts to dominate the individual. How can this be done? Practice these exercises repeatedly:
    ➢ Prohibit negative thoughts.
    ➢ Choose topics that are positive or neutral. For example, think about pleasant experiences from the past; people whom you admire; fun friends; or episodes from some

book or a special film. Consider these things while you do your routine tasks or substitute them for the thoughts that cause concern.

➢ Have constructive concerns as a motivation. To solve the problems that provoke stress, it is necessary to think about alternatives, other possibilities, and ways to overcome a difficulty, instead of immersing oneself in destructive, repetitive, and obsessive worry.

➢ Discard irrational beliefs. People sometimes have negative ideas and beliefs regarding themselves and the environment in which they live. These negative thought patterns increase stress. For example, they may think: "I am good for nothing"; "No one likes my company"; "Happiness comes along by chance, and my time has not come along yet"; or "My supervisor hates me and only wants to make my life difficult." These ideas must be rejected. And if someone is not able to do this alone, he or she should seek the help of a psychotherapist to talk about this matter and free themselves from these irrational beliefs.

• *Physical plan*—Physical exercise is the best medication against stress. If your health allows, do vigorous physical exercise (running, swimming, team sports), or walk fast every day.

Relaxing is another good solution: dedicate half an hour daily to rest (not to sleep); tense up the muscles one by one, alternating with moments of complete relaxation after each tightening of the muscle.

Occasional deep breathing is also very useful to fight stress: take a deep breath, expanding the abdomen (not the lungs), and hold the air for a few seconds before exhaling.

• *Spiritual plan*—Mental and emotional peace are incompatible with stress. A calm conscience can be obtained through faith and prayer.

The Lord Jesus, after an exhausting day of sermons, walking, and pressure from the crowd, said to His disciples: "Come with me by yourselves to a quiet place and get some rest" (Mark 6:31). His method included getting up in the early morning hours, when it was still dark, and going to a quiet place to pray (Mark 1:35).

Spend time studying the Bible—at least fifteen to twenty minutes, and end with a prayer to God. Thank Him for His message and ask Him for strength to face the difficulties caused by the stress. It is also beneficial to read the experience of some Bible character and seek inspiration in his or her story.

Look in the Bible for the incredible stories of Abraham, Jacob, Joseph, Moses, Samuel, Jonathan, David, Samson, Jonah, Esther, Elijah, Peter, Paul and, above all, the life of Jesus and His teachings. Learn the magnificent lessons of these people. You will find that reading and reflecting on these subjects drives away stress.

Practice Total Health

The best way to protect yourself against stress is to adopt a healthy and balanced lifestyle, in relation to the body as well as the mind. Maintaining good physical and mental health is within the reach of everyone.

One caution that we should take is with obsessive thoughts. Have you ever felt incapable of stopping a thought? Seek to free yourself from this threat by observing the following steps:

- Identify the thoughts that cause you anxiety or stress.
- At the first indication of the possibility of undesirable thoughts, say (or shout out loud, if necessary): "ENOUGH, STOP!"
- Try to distract yourself by filling your mind with uplifting thoughts—a Bible verse, an enjoyable memory, and so on.

Always cultivate a positive attitude toward all things, and occupy your mind with pleasant and constructive subjects. Understand that only when this control technique becomes a habit will you be able to banish from your mind undesirable thoughts in an instinctive and secure manner.

- *Environment.* Your environment also plays a large part—especially noise and sound pollution. When it rises above the limit of possible risk (60 decibels), sound can become a great stress agent. If the volume is increased, it is capable of causing lesions in the ear and the loss of hearing ability. Excess noise can also provoke psychophysical alterations: tiredness, irritability, insomnia, headache, muscle tension. All of these symptoms are associated with stress.

- *Diet and food.* The best foods are those that remain nearest to their natural state. Whole-grain cereals prepared simply (such as brown rice) or homemade items (such as bread) make up the basis of humanity's traditional foods. Vegetables, fruit, legumes, and nuts are also necessary because of their healing and nutritional properties. Food of animal origin, such as meat, fish, and dairy products and their fats may not be the best options for good nutrition.

- *Water.* Water is the best drink possible for human beings and the one that best renews fluids in the body. Experts recommend that you drink water in abundance daily (on an average, six to eight glasses, and not at mealtimes). Other widely used drinks, such as carbonated beverages, beer, or coffee, are a burden to the body, which then needs to eliminate the toxic substances from the alcohol, or the caffeine and the dyes, besides storing the excess sugars as fat. This can end up obstructing the blood vessels and cause various types of vascular and cardiovascular diseases.

- *Exercise*. All organs and systems in the body were created for activity. Within your limits and under your doctor's recommendation, exercise your muscles and bones for your well-being and regeneration. Make the effort and practice some sport or hobby that provides physical exercise, or walk regularly.
- *Harmful substances.* The substances referred to as psychoactive (alcohol, tobacco, and other mind-altering drugs) directly affect the central nervous system and consequently the mood and the capacity to rationalize. A prevention plan or plan for a cure from stress will completely eliminate the use of sub- stances that alter mental functions.
- *Rest*. After physical work comes restoring rest. It is important to have a balance between physical tiredness and the hours of sleep. Respecting the seven to eight hours of sleep that the majority of adults need is a task of great importance for stress prevention. Without proper rest, it is not possible for you to face the tasks of work, and this will produce anxiety and stress. Besides rest at night, it is important to take a vacation once in a while and disconnect from work. We need daily rest and annual rest. But also, many people have forgotten the important principle of a weekly rest.

Anti-Stress Day

The fourth commandment in the law of God states the following: "Remember the Sabbath day by keeping it holy. Six days you shall labor and do all your work, but the seventh day is a Sabbath to the Lord your God. On it you shall not do any work, neither you, nor your son or daughter, nor your male or female servant, your animals, nor any foreigner residing in your towns. For in six days, the Lord made the heavens and the earth, the sea, and all that is in them, but he rested on the seventh day. Therefore, the Lord blessed the Sabbath day and made it holy" (Exodus 20:8–11).

Unfortunately, this most-forgotten commandment is the one that begins with the word *remember*. It would do so much good for Paul, Laura, and Carlos—and in reality, for any person—to reserve one day per week for physical, mental, and spiritual rest. Do you know why? Because we were created to function in a cycle of seven days. This is called circaseptan rhythm.

God's recommendations always aim for our well-being. When He placed a specific commandment in His law regarding the sanctification of one day, He was warning us about the race in search of possessions and the physical and mental deterioration that comes from it. Today, we can say that by obeying the fourth commandment, we are actually improving our quality of life and avoiding stress. Additionally, we are following the law of life itself, because, after all, the Creator of physical and biological laws is the same Creator of spiritual laws.

When we go to the Bible, we notice that the Sabbath is present from the beginning to the end of its pages. At the beginning of life on this planet, we read in Genesis 2:1–3 that the Creator Himself did three things on the seventh day: He blessed it, He sanctified it, and He rested on it. When God sanctifies something, He sets it aside for a specific and holy purpose. When He blesses something or someone, no one can remove this blessing.

You may ask: Is it possible for God to become tired? Isaiah 40:28 tells us He does not. After all, He is the Almighty. In a similar way, Jesus did not need to be baptized because He did not have any sin, but He did it to give us an example (Matthew 3:13–15). In the same manner, God gave us an example by resting on the seventh day. Additionally, this rest (*shabbath*, in Hebrew) has more to do with a pause in His creative activity.

57

In Mark 2:27, Jesus said that the Sabbath is a present given to "man" (the human being), not to a people or specific group. When the Sabbath was inaugurated on Earth, only Adam and Eve were living at the time (also read Isaiah 56:6, 7). There were no Jews or any other ethnic groups of people. Exodus 20:8–11, Leviticus 23:3, and Matthew 28:1 make it clear that the Sabbath is the seventh day, and not any other day of the week. And Ezekiel 20:12 and 20 show that the Sabbath is a sign of the creature's fidelity toward his or her Creator. The Sabbath is a memorial of Creation, a temple in time.

Clearly, Jesus, the Word incarnated (John 1:1–3), observed the Sabbath when He was here on Earth (see Luke 4:16). The same attitude was followed by His disciples (Acts 16:13; 17:2). Adam and Eve, the patriarchs, the prophets, and Jesus's followers always sanctified the seventh day of the week, which, according to the Bible, begins at sunset on Friday (the day of preparation) and continues until the following sunset (Nehemiah 13:19; Genesis 1:19; Mark 1:32; Leviticus 23:32). Marking the change of a day at midnight is a human invention that goes against the natural human biorhythm.

"If you keep your feet from breaking the Sabbath and from doing as you please on my holy day, if you call the Sabbath a delight and the Lord's holy day honorable, and if you honor it by not going your own way and not doing as you please or speaking idle words, then you will find your joy in the Lord, and I will cause you to ride in triumph on the heights of the land and to feast on the inheritance of your father Jacob" (Isaiah 58:13, 14). This is how God wants us to keep His holy day—a practice that will last for eternity (Isaiah 66:22, 23).

The Sabbath is a present from God each week. Unwrap this present!

How to Make the Sabbath a Delight

- Make plans to usher in the Sabbath early in the week.
- Look forward to the Sabbath as a special day of communion with Jesus.
- At sunset on Friday, gather your family, sing, pray, and usher in the beginning of the Sabbath together.
- On Sabbath morning, go to church as Jesus did.
- Beforehand, prepare a special and delicious meal for lunch on Sabbath.
- In the afternoon, if there are small children in the family, plan an outing to a park or similar location where they can talk about the power and love of God demonstrated in nature.
- Become involved in service activities and offer physical and moral support to the needy, as Jesus did.
- At sunset on Saturday, gather the family once again to pray and bid farewell to the Sabbath, asking for God's blessings on the new week that is beginning.

Test Yourself

To learn whether your stress is causing you harm, answer YES or NO to the following questions:

1. Do you enjoy nature in your free time? _____
2. Do you drink alcoholic beverages? _____
3. Do you eat fruit and vegetables in abundance? _____
4. Do you smoke? _____
5. Do you exercise regularly? _____
6. Do you use sedatives habitually? _____
7. Do you live in a clean and organized house? _____
8. Do you live in a noisy neighborhood? _____
9. Does your home have a cozy atmosphere? _____
10. Are you always surrounded by many people? _____
11. Do you have a good appetite? _____
12. Do you forget things easily? _____
13. Does your digestive system function well? _____
14. Do you feel tired for no apparent reason? _____

15. Do you sleep well? _____
16. Do you become irritated easily? _____
17. Do you have a good relationship with your superiors? _____
18. Do you use your car as your means of transportation? _____
19. Do you have steady work? _____
20. Do you take work home with you? _____
21. Do you have good relationships with your colleagues and friends? _____
22. Do you become very impatient when you have to wait for someone? _____
23. Do you know how to listen patiently? _____
24. Do you talk a lot? _____
25. Are you satisfied with your sex life? _____
26. Do you attempt to do things better than others? _____
27. Are you satisfied with the way you are? _____
28. Are you a perfectionist? _____
29. Do you have a sense of humor? _____
30. Do you become irritated when you have to wait in line? _____

Scoring:

Check the answers to the odd-numbered questions and give yourself 1 point for each NO.

Check the answers to the even-numbered questions and give yourself 1 point for each YES.

Total: _____

Results:

From 0 to 7 points

You are well protected against stress. Perhaps you need to make a little change to obtain even better motivation in your life.

From 8 to 13 points

You have a medium level of stress. Things can go in one direction or the other. It is important to adopt preventative measures against too much stress now.

From 14 points and beyond

This is a warning of high stress in your life and a call for you to make an examination of your lifestyle habits, the environment in which you live, your mental attitude, and your relationships, and make plans to improve them all.

5

Psychological
Traumas

Joseph, a young Hebrew who lived almost two thousand years before Christ, was born into a good family, and he soon demonstrated intelligence and vision. Motivated by jealousy, his brothers sold him as a slave to the residents of another country. In his new situation, Joseph had to suffer in silence and adapt to the conditions, which were totally opposite of what he was accustomed to. He experienced traumatic situations of intense stress. However, he emerged honorably from these difficult tests, even reaching the highest of positions in Egypt.

How was Joseph able to preserve his mental health in the midst of such adversity? Joseph exercised his faith in God during many years of trials; he asked his Creator for strength to overcome such oppression; he prayed daily and maintained contact with God in moments of anguish. Above all else, he kept alive the hope that someday his pain would pass and God reserved a happy ending for his life.

Joseph decided to act as an agent of change. He had every reason not to forgive, to charge unpayable emotional interest and to collect equally unpayable emotional interest, but he decided to repay all those involved in a completely different manner than the treatment he had received. The complete story is recorded in the book of Genesis, chapters 37 and 39–50.

Intense, emotionally charged events, especially if experienced at a difficult time in life or at an early age, can cause depression in the individual. Examples include a child who is ridiculed or suffers insults; is startled in the dark; is frightened by snakes or spiders; feels slandered; is coerced for sexual satisfaction; or loses a father or mother at a young age. In the same way that a serious physical accident leaves permanent marks, emotional traumas can leave aftereffects for many years.

The most visible consequences are manifested during the initial days and weeks following the experience—reoccurring dreams, passing memories, denial, anxiety, or lack of attention and concentration. In some cases, especially in children, the aftereffects can be permanent, becoming a strong barrier for a healthy mental life.

Traumas and tensions may even develop into an illness. "Animal studies have demonstrated that social, behavioral, and environmental factors can actually determine whether genes are expressed—that is, whether they are turned on or off. For example, stress has been shown to cause symptoms of diabetes, such as hyperglycemia, in animals that are genetically susceptible to diabetes. Animals not exposed to stress conditions were less likely to develop hyperglycemia or diabetes, even though they were genetically prone to the disorder," wrote Norman B. Anderson in the book *Emotional Longevity: What Really Determines How Long You Live*.[1]

Effects of Past Traumas

Traumas from the past can produce:

- *Insecurity.* The individual self receives a large part of the traumatizing impact, and the person loses confidence in himself or herself, demonstrating insecurity.

- *Difficulty in accomplishing normal activities.* The affected individual feels incapable of attaining simple objectives. For example, young women or girls who have been victims of sexual abuse usually have difficulties in relating socially to young men. Or the boy whose older brothers frightened him with a spider can develop a phobia of spiders.
- *Paranoiac tendencies.* The traumatized person demonstrates mistrust in the environment and can interpret neutral attitudes of other individuals as a trap against him or her and consider himself or herself as a victim of aggression or undue persecution.
- *Depression.* The traumatizing event usually is perceived as a loss (loss of honor, loss of a beloved person or pet), and all loss brings with it the risk of depressive symptoms.
- *Anorexia and bulimia.* There is also a clear correlation between being a victim of sexual abuse and ending up with eating disorders, especially anorexia and bulimia.

How to Overcome Traumas

There are traumas that, because of their seriousness, require psychiatric treatment. Others, although without such drastic consequences, have a tendency to complicate the development of the individual's life within normality. For this, we offer the following counsel:

- *Accept the past and focus on the future.* If you get stuck dwelling on the past, you cannot look toward the future with the necessary trust. Additionally, it is good to remember that our mind does not have a perfect ability for registering data. Our memories are reconstructed events from the past, and these memories are affected by our feelings and by the comprehension that we have of them in the present.

- *Talk about the traumatic event.* In a secure environment, talking (or writing) about the event that caused the trauma is a very important step. Look for a trustworthy person and tell him or her what happened. Group therapy is helpful for people who have experienced trauma. Hurts that cannot be stated will not be forgotten.
- *Look at the positive side.* Disasters and calamities tend to unite survivors, families, and communities. Be grateful for the care demonstrated toward those who face tragedies. Additionally, when traumatic situations are faced courageously, they tend to strengthen the character of those who go through the experience.
- *Forgive.* Although it is a process that can take a long time, forgiveness releases us from hate and resentment toward those responsible for the trauma. This is an important step toward resolution, and it is also applicable to ourselves— self- forgiveness and self-reconciliation. Resolving hate does not prohibit the victim from wanting a just conclusion to the traumatic experience.

Hurt and resentment make us prisoners of the past and continually remind us of what happened long ago. Truly, the person most affected by resentment is yourself.

Forgiveness, however, is not always spontaneous, because our capacity to love (to forgive is to love) is limited. Seek the Source of forgiveness—the God of love—who, according to the gospel, wants us to be His friends and can facilitate overcoming the past that overshadows us. Remember what the Lord's Prayer states: "Forgive our debts, as we also have forgiven our debtors" (Matthew 6:12).

Write Down the Experiences

Melanie Greenberg and Arthur Stone carried out an interesting study at State University of New York at Stony Brook. A total of sixty university students participated, sharing their past experiences in the following steps:

1. The scientists grouped the participants into subgroups: those who had experienced a severe trauma, those who had lived through a low-severity trauma, and those who had not suffered any trauma.
2. Some participants were asked to reveal their experience in writing, and others were not given this opportunity, so that they could serve as a point of reference or as a control group.
3. During the following months, the health and disease tendencies of all participants were observed.

The results demonstrated that those who had gone through a severe trauma and revealed it in writing experienced much greater progress in physical health than those who had not written anything about their traumatic experience.[2]

Studies such as this demonstrate that revealing a traumatic experience is not only good for the soul but also for the body. One individual who supports this idea is the author and Nazi concentration camp survivor, Elie Wiesel. He wrote and re- wrote his experiences of personal trauma, and through this he was able to find meaning and the significance of these trau- mas. Even if we are still not able to express our feelings and memories in an appropriate manner, we should still try.

Additionally, in the struggle to overcome trauma, it is essential for us to avoid self-victimization, but rather to look for comfort in religion, to create new objectives in life (perhaps even use the experience itself to do something good for other people), and to not nurture the desire for revenge or hate.

One last biblical counsel in this context is this: "One thing I do: Forgetting what is behind and straining toward what is ahead, I press on toward the goal" (Philippians 3:13, 14).

Resilience

The word *resilience* comes from physics and describes the capacity of some material to return to their original state or even improve their quality after they have been submitted to extreme situations. In human terms, resilience is the capacity of a person to recover emotional equilibrium or even to become stronger after going through a traumatic situation.

Evidently there are different levels of resilience, and they vary from person to person. What traumatizes one individual may not necessarily affect another person so much. This depends on such factors as temperament, capacity to resolve problems, intelligence, self-esteem, social competence, self-control, family and social ties.

We cannot overemphasize the importance of good relationships. A study of 724 people throughout a period of more than seventy years concluded that wealth and fame do not guarantee happiness, neither do longevity or resilience. In reality, good relationships with family and friends extend life and make it more pleasant. Robert J. Waldinger, psychiatrist and professor at the Harvard School of Medicine, coordinates this study currently. He cites three important lessons regarding relationships taken from this study in the United States:

(1) social connections benefit human beings, while loneliness kills; (2) the quality of relationships is more important than the quantity; and (3) happy, long-lasting relationships protect physical and mental health.[3]

"The experience of loneliness turns out to be toxic. People who are more isolated than they want to be from others find that they are less happy, their health declines earlier in midlife, their brain functioning declines sooner and they live shorter lives than people who are not lonely," states Waldinger in a TED Talk available on YouTube.[4] But there is another factor as important as, or perhaps more important than, good social relationships.

Researchers today recognize that an important factor for the development and strengthening of resilience is religion. Besides providing a network of social support, religion provides a positive vision of the future. However, it cannot be just any religion, suggests psychiatrist Harold Koenig, who studies the relationship between religiosity and health at Duke University in North Carolina. He affirms that it is of no value for the individual to simply state that he or she is "spiritual" and not have a practical religious experience. It is vital to be *committed* to religion in order to enjoy its benefits. It is essential to attend worship services and express faith at home and in other locations through prayer and Bible study. He asserts that religious belief needs to influence one's life so that it may also influence one's health.

In an article in the magazine *Vida e Saúde* [*Life and Health*], Dr. Koenig explained that religious involvement reduces psychological stress, which decreases inflammation and the rate of telomere shortening in cells. He explained, "Telomeres are a biological clock for the cell. They shorten at each cell division, and when they are gone, the cell dies and organ degeneration occurs."[5] This explains why religious people live an average of seven to fourteen years longer, according to research.

Remember: religion will only be favorable if it is positive and focused on a good relationship with God and one's fellow human beings. The Bible describes true religion in this way: "Religion that God our Father accepts as pure and faultless is this: to look after orphans and widows in their distress and to keep oneself from being polluted by the world" (James 1:27).

In this world, it is impossible to eliminate all traumatic situations. As resilient as a person may be, suffering knocks at their door and brings pain along with it. Why do things have to be like that?

The World is a Battlefield

The Bible makes it clear that this world is a battlefield, and the conflict began far from here, in heaven. Ezekiel 28:13–19 and Isaiah 14:12–14 describe what ignited this conflict: pride and vanity. Lucifer was a perfect angel created by God; a type of chief angel, he was loved and respected by all. At some point in time, in a way beyond our understanding, jealousy began to emerge in his angelic heart, and he wanted the position that belonged only to the Creator. As a child of God, he had everything, but he decided that he would no longer offer reverence to the Eternal One and began to question the divine government and the law on which this government was based.

Knowing the character of God revealed in the Holy Scriptures, we can imagine that the Father tried everything to convince His child to repent of his sins and abandon the rebellion. But Lucifer decided to go forward with his plans, finally reaching the point of no return—the point at which the sinner no longer cares about sin and feels no desire to repent. His heart hardened to the appeals of the Holy Spirit.

Revelation 5:11 states that billions of angels exist. Many of them joined Lucifer's rebellion. Was God really a tyrant, as Lucifer accused Him of being? Wasn't the fact that He had laws that should be obeyed by His creatures proof that He was arbitrary? For the opposing angel, it was as if God's law was an unjust obligation.

Some people ask themselves: If the omniscient God knew of Lucifer's feelings from the beginning, why not destroy him before the controversy spread? Consider for a moment that for the heavenly angels this was a new experience; they had never experienced the thoughts and feelings now crossing their minds. There were doubts in heaven for the first time. If God had destroyed the rebel angel right at the beginning, what type of feeling could this have awakened in the other created beings? "Oh, so this is how things work here. You disobey, you die?" Do you see? The Creator had to allow the consequences of the rebellion to be known so all angels could make their choice and decide under which government they would like to live. He also offered an opportunity for the rebel to return to the right path of his own free will, but Lucifer finally decided not to do this.

Others go further and question: "Couldn't God have created a universe where there was no evil?" Let's try to explain this with another question: Could God create a square wheel? This does not make sense because the Creator does not violate His laws, and He does not work with illogical impossibilities. Therefore, to create a universe with beings that are endowed with the ability to choose, God needed to run risks. This is because a universe cannot exist with freedom without having the possibility of a choice for evil. God did not want to create automated beings—robots programmed to obey. God is love (1 John 4:8), and He wants to be loved. So it is important to remember that love is only manifested where there is freedom. No one can be forced to love.

Could God have created a universe without the potential for evil? Yes, but not *this* universe. Therefore, different from what some say, evil does not prove that the Creator does not exist. It proves exactly the opposite: that He exists and that He endowed us with the freedom to choose. Besides, if God did not exist, the definition of evil itself would lose all its meaning. After all, evil is the opposite of good. Without a moral absolute to serve as a parameter, how could what is good be determined? We only know that a line is crooked because we compare it to a straight line.

Unfortunately, one-third of the heavenly angels joined with Lucifer (later called Satan, or the enemy) and were expelled from heaven (Revelation 12:3, 4, 7, 9), ending up on our planet. Here, Satan used deceit to involve Adam and Eve in his rebellion (Genesis 3:1–6). With much satanic cunning and intelligence, the enemy was able to inject Eve with the virus of his own rebellion. He suggested that if she disobeyed God, she would become a superior creature, reaching equality with her Creator. Lucifer was the one who wanted this! And he was able to convince the woman that she wanted it too.

The original lie could be summarized into two statements: (1) you will not die and (2) you will become like God. From then until now, the enemy has been disseminating this same lie under various disguises, all with the objective of distancing humanity from the Creator. Upon considering themselves as immortal and self-sufficient, people will leave off recognizing their dependence on the Source of life. With this, the rebel wounds the heart of the Father.

Because of this, we can say that this planet is a battlefield. Continually, good and evil angels dispute their influence over us. We should always remind ourselves that "our struggle is not against flesh and blood, but against the rulers, against the authorities, against the powers of this dark world and against the spiritual forces of evil in the heavenly realms" (Ephesians 6:12).

In a war, there are always traumatic situations. If you're in doubt, ask a former soldier who has gone to battle. In spite of everything, our General is personally engaged in our salvation, even though we have to experience one war injury or another. Additionally, the General has already announced the end of all battles, on the occasion of His return.

How can we be certain that the General is really interested in us and did not abandon us in a minefield, leaving us without hope? It is simple. When Satan was able to involve Adam and Eve in the rebellion, he thought he had placed the Creator in checkmate. After all, the couple knew that the "wages of sin is death" (Romans 6:23). Since they had sinned, both deserved to die forever. If God destroyed them, the enemy would say something like this to all created beings: "Did you see? Didn't I tell you that He is a tyrant and He is evil?" However, being aware of divine mercy, the fallen angel expected that God would overlook the attitude of disobedience of the transgressing couple. In that case, Satan could accuse the Creator of being incoherent and unfaithful to His own word. If He could ignore the guilt of the two humans, why not Satan's own guilt?

However, the rebel did not count on something surprising, which left him speechless. Yes, "the wages of sin is death," and someone must experience eternal death because of this, but it would not be Adam and Eve. God, in the person of Jesus, would die in the place of the sinner, assuming his or her guilt, and reveal in a grand manner the extent to which the General was willing to go because of His love for His children.

It is for this reason that He has a moral authority to say, "Come to me, all you who are weary and burdened, and I will give you rest" (Matthew 11:28).

Neither Paul nor Laura nor Carlos, nor you or any other person, can change what has happened in the past. The war injuries are there on your body, in your mind, and on your heart. There is one thing, however, they can do, and you can do: change your attitude in relation to the things that took place before in the battles of life. Change the way you face these traumas.

The individual who trusts in the God of the Bible knows that "in all things God works for the good of those who love him" (Romans 8:28). Then, understand and accept that it is not God who originated evil. He uses these experiences from the battlefield to contribute toward your growth and your eternal salvation.

Trust in the Father. Trust in the General. He has already proven that He is worthy of this trust.

---

1. Norman B. Anderson with P. Elizabeth Anderson, *Emotional Longevity: What Really Determines How Long You Live* (New York: Viking, 2003), P. 5.
2. Julián Melgosa, "Cicatrizes" ["Scars"], *Saúde e Lar*, January 2015, http://www.saudelar.com/edicoes/2015/janeiro/principal.asp?send=10_psicologia.htm.

3. Márcio Tonetti, "Segredo da Felicidade e da Longevidade" ["Secret of Happiness and Longevity"], *Revista Adventista*, February 17, 2016, http://www.revistaadventista.com.br/blog/2016/02/17/segredo-da-felicidade-e-da-longevidade/.
4. Robert Waldinger, "What Makes a Good Life? Lessons From the Longest Study on Happiness." Speech at TEDx Conference, November 2015, https://www.youtube.com/watch?v=8KkKuTCFvzI.
5. Michelson Borges, "Saúde Emocional e Espiritual" ["Emotional and Spiritual Health"], *Vida e Saúde* [*Life and Health*], June 2015, pp. 8–13.

6

Enslaved
by Addictions

There is something more that we need to mention about Laura and the reason why she decided to remain single: she does not trust men. This is not only because of the negative experience she had with her father in her childhood, losing the one who should have been her male role model, but also because she knows men who do not deserve her trust. Laura knows that the majority of men are involved with some type of pornography. How could she have a relationship with a man who possibly would be comparing her with supposedly perfect actresses? How could she accept someone as a husband whose heart has been stained by perverted sex?

"Friends" of our friend Paul tried to convince him that it would be good for him and his marriage to watch some of "those films." However, he knew the cause of the coldness in his marriage. It was not the lack of something erotic or something "spicy" but the lack of love, companionship, and dialog—things day-to-day stress was stealing from him.

Besides this, how could he watch pornography and then look into the pure eyes of his two little children, especially his little girl, who enjoyed writing sweet love letters to him? One day his daughter would grow up, and he could never conceive the idea that she could end up being treated as a sexual object in front of cameras, just for the enjoyment of an audience with lustful eyes and dirty minds. Fortunately, Paul was among the minority of men who avoided pornography.

The problem becomes even more serious when we realize that children have easy access to pornography. According to an analysis of 3.5 million searches on the Internet between 2008 and 2009, the words *sex* and *porn* were among the ten most searched for by kids.[1]

Effects of Porn Consumption

A study carried out by Padua University[2] in Italy found that seventy percent of young men who sought out neurologists because of unsatisfactory sexual performance admitted to frequently viewing pornography on the Internet. Other behavioral studies suggest that the loss of libido takes place because individuals who spend a great amount of time viewing pornography are suppressing the brain's natural response to pleasure. Years substituting the natural limits of libido for intense stimulation will result in damage to these men's response to dopamine. This neurotransmitter is behind desire, motivation, and addictions. It directs the search for rewards. Once pleasure is strongly linked to pornography, real sex seems to no longer offer a reward. So this would be the cause for the lack of desire in many men.

In his book *Wired for Intimacy: How Pornography Hijacks the Male Brain*, William Struthers of Wheaton College draws on neuroscience to explain why pornography is so addictive to the male mind. It's all about *intimacy*: men seek everything from pornography to prostitutes in their pursuit of satisfying their deepest emotional needs. "They are driven to seek out sexual intimacy," he says.[3]

According to Struthers, viewing pornographic images creates new patterns in the brain's wiring, and the habit reinforces the rewiring.[4] At this point, the comparison to the addictive effects of drug consumption becomes unavoidable: "Tolerance is when, as a result of exposure to the substance, the body adjusts so that later exposure to the same levels of the substance results in a lesser effect. If I take the same dose of a drug over and over and my body begins to tolerate it, I will need to take a higher dose of the drug in order for it to have the same effect that it did with a lower dose the first time."[5] Therefore, sex addiction "acts as a polydrug, delivering emotional and sensory excitation and energizing a man sexually."[6]

How to Identify Sexual Addiction

If you observe in yourself, your spouse, or a friend or family member two, three, or more of the following behaviors, this could indicate a case of sexual addiction. You should speak to the individual in a calm manner, without accusations, and with an attitude of assistance:

1. An individual insists on staying in front of the computer or television when no one is home or everyone else is asleep.

2. An individual keeps a small case, backpack, drawer, or closet with a key, and no one in the family or at work can have access to this location.

3. An individual contemplates members of the opposite sex for a long time after they pass by.

4. An individual receives charges on their credit card for which they have no explanation.

5. An individual arrives very late from work or is absent more than necessary, using travel and professional obligations as a justification.

6. When the individual is on the Internet and someone comes near, the individual quickly changes the screen.

7. The individual does not have sexual relations with their spouse, or desires it in extravagant ways.

8. The individual is emotionally distant from their spouse.

9. The individual seems to be absent and distracted even at the most intimate moments.

10. The individual demonstrates an abrupt change in mood and threatening behavior.

How to Overcome Sexual Addiction

The psychological process is similar to any other addiction. Much advice for chemical dependence is also valid for sexual addiction:

1. The first step is to admit the problem and demonstrate a willingness to correct this behavior.
2. Seek the support of another individual. The best person is the spouse of the addict (under the guidance of a specialist). If this is not possible, then it could be a friend or close family member.
3. Always be vigilant (do not stay alone for very long; continue planned activities).
4. Maintain absolute sexual sobriety; engage in sex only with one's spouse.
5. Make use of structured help mechanisms; block certain environments on the Internet and limit the time of Internet access.
6. Plan recreational activities, preferably outdoors and in different locations from the usual.
7. This tendency could have its origin in sexual abuse in childhood or in a troubled childhood. In this case, the plan of rehabilitation should be accompanied by formal psychotherapy to go deeper into matters of the past and eliminate conflicts.
8. For the support individual: be compassionate and treat the addict as someone who is ill, who needs to recover. He or she needs to accept his or her responsibility. Once responsibility has been taken and the individual has decided to become accountable, he or she should not be blamed or criticized excessively for the unacceptable conduct. The addict needs compassion, sympathy, and support.

Addicted to Cigarettes

In many countries the use of cigarettes has decreased. However, in some countries cigarette smoking continues to rise. It is especially popular among young people. Nicotine has a high power to cause addiction and represents a barrier for giving up this habit. If you want to stop smoking, follow these steps:

1. *Examine your habits.* Are there particular objects or situations that increase your desire to smoke? Reconsider these circumstances and avoid them, or prepare yourself to resist: when you go to bed, get up, have breakfast, are at a gathering with friends, when you sit in your favorite chair, when you are alone someplace, when you finish a meal, etc. Avoid smoking in these situations.

2. *Look for new environments.* Change your schedule, your meetings and customary locations. Participate in healthy activities outdoors and in environments that are relaxing.

3. *Include your friends and family.* Tell all of them that you have decided to stop smoking. They will support you. If possible, join someone who also wants to give up the habit, and when you meet, encouragement can be both given and received.

4. *Watch your diet.* Detoxification should be accompanied by many fruits and vegetables. Drink lots of water and citrus fruit juices. This will help to eliminate the nicotine from your system, and your desire for cigarettes will gradually decrease.

5. *Exercise.* Physical exercise will relax the tension of detoxification and will encourage a positive mood.

6. *Give yourself a reward.* Establish compensations after several days of success—go to a special place or buy an article of clothing with the money you have saved from not smoking.

7. *Seek support in the spiritual dimension.* Many addicts disregard this step and are unsuccessful in their attempt to quit. Pray to God as though you were talking to a friend and ask for strength to overcome this habit.

Dangerous Caffeine

Many think that caffeine is not a drug. However, the psychiatric manual DSM-5 considers caffeine intoxication at the point when an individual ingests 250 milligrams or more in a single day (for example: more than two to three cups of drip-brewed coffee). "Energy" drinks can have more caffeine than coffee.[7] The effects of consumption of caffeine are restlessness, nervousness, insomnia, diuresis, flushed face, muscle twitching, gastrointestinal disturbance, rambling flow of thought and speech, tachycardia, and psychomotor agitation.[8]

The following products contain varying quantities of caffeine:[9]

Product	Size	Caffeine
Black tea	8 oz. / 237 mL	14–70 mg
Cola soft drinks	12 oz. / 355 mL	23–40 mg
Dark chocolate–coated coffee beans	28 pieces	336 mg
Energy drinks	8 oz. / 237 mL	70–100 mg
Espresso, restaurant-style	1 oz. / 30 mL	47–75 mg
Instant coffee	8 oz. / 237 mL	27–173 mg

Vicious Circle

Happiness has been defined as the total absence of addiction. This includes addictions to "heavy" or illegal drugs, compulsive sex, gambling, video games, and the Internet. It also includes common substances that cause addictions, such as alcohol, cigarettes, and coffee. These substances are called psychoactive because they affect mental function. In addition, some people are addicted to such things as diets, medications, or even physical exercise.

The vicious circle of drugs is very dangerous. Whether they are legal or illegal, or contain chemical components or not, they bring harm to one's health. All addictions take away the freedom of those who suffer from this dependence. Furthermore, they cause very serious risks:

- *Dependence*. Drugs or chemical dependence create the desire to continue usage. The more that the individual satisfies this desire, the greater the desire becomes for further usage.

- *Tolerance.* The drug user needs larger and larger doses to obtain effects similar to prior use.
- *Abstinence syndrome.* Addicts can feel a psychological state of extreme agitation when they do not have access to the desired substance or cannot carry out the desired behavior. It can also be a physical experience; the body is habituated to the substance and cannot obtain the dosage desired. Abstinence symptoms include: insomnia, agitation, heart palpitations, perspiration, nausea, vomiting, and others.
- *Effects on the brain (in chemical dependence).* Drugs attack the central nervous system. When an addictive substance reaches the brain, several vital functions are altered, and the individual becomes incapable of accomplishing simple mental activities. When consumption takes place over a long period, irreversible lesions can develop.

The first three risks are not only associated with the chemically dependent but also relate to individuals addicted to certain behaviors. The individual addicted to pornography, for example, feels a strong desire to repeat the activity. After a certain time, the images viewed are not sufficient, and the individual needs stronger or more obscene images. The lack of availability of the images will produce extreme agitation or frustration in the addict.

How to Prevent Addictions

The majority of addicts, especially those addicted to substances, begin initial use when they are preteens or teenagers. For this reason, preventive measures should be focused on these age-groups. Beginning with their first years in school, children should receive instruction regarding drugs and their risks. School programs should have a place for talks and seminars presented by relevant individuals (former addicts, doctors, lawyers, psychologists, police officers, social workers, etc.).

As a matter of principle, all schools and other learning institutions should be declared drug-free areas, adopting measures to avoid becoming centers for drug trafficking or locations where children and teens are introduced to drugs.

The parents of children and young people also have a responsibility in prevention. They should talk about the problem, adopting the following strategies:

- Have a firm and coherent position regarding drugs and addictions.
- Mold healthy self-esteem in their children.
- Maintain a stable and safe home environment.
- Demonstrate flexibility in opinions and behavior, yet maintain well-defined limits.
- Give an irreproachable example with regard to addictions.

Authorities also have an important role in educating against addictions and in favor of total health: attractive and persuasive programs, the use of legal precautions (for example: necessary labeling on alcoholic beverages and on cigarettes), rules that regulate the sale and distribution, and so on. It is extremely important to suppress drug trafficking in schools and other institutions and locations where children and young people gather.

When it comes to other addictions (work, sex, gambling), these may continue into adulthood. It is indispensable to remember that with these addictions, as well as chemical dependence, anxiety frequently adds to the problem. For this reason, one way to prevent involvement in an addiction is to overcome anxiety.

How to Overcome Addictions

It has been proven that the individual cannot give up addictions on their own. The addict needs social, professional, and spiritual support. For this reason, the advice presented here is especially directed toward the family or to the addict's support system:

- If the addict has made many attempts already to give up the addiction, he or she should be encouraged to seek a rehabilitation center.
- Support the plan established by the center or the qualified professional. Trust in the treatment, and encourage the addict (child, spouse, friend, etc.).
- Avoid overprotection and enabling. It is a great temptation to protect the people we love. However, in these circumstances it is necessary to remain firm regarding the treatment.
- Reward accomplishments. The addict needs external reinforcement to reach new objectives. Rewards can include food, films, outings, games, books, or visits, according to preferences and circumstances.
- Prepare a calm, healthy, and adequate environment to keep the addict far from the atmosphere that facilitates the addiction (locations, people, objects, etc.), because triggers can lead the addict into a relapse.

Support groups are excellent methods for overcoming addictions. For example, Alcoholics Anonymous (AA), Narcotics Anonymous (NA), Gamblers Anonymous (GA), and Sex and Love Addicts Anonymous (SLAA) have high rates of success among participants. The addict, in meeting with others who suffer from the same problem, will strive with greater persistence. It is imperative to recognize that the power addiction holds over a person is so great that many overcome only through God's help. The success of Alcoholics Anonymous (AA) is due in part to human support, demonstrated by the experience of former alcoholics, and to God's support, who is accepted by those who through faith are willing to receive Him. After attaining initial success, the struggle does not end, because the risk of relapse is very high. Therefore, it is important to carefully plan the return to normality by observing the following areas:

- *Employment.* The rehabilitated individual may need a new job, with new colleagues and with a firm purpose toward reintegration, without falling back into the addiction.
- *Social atmosphere.* For a long period in recovery, the rehabilitated individual needs someone who continues to carefully and firmly observe his or her environment. He or she should have relationships with people who know how to enjoy life without the use of chemical substances or other addictions, living simply and naturally.
- *Leisure time.* Free time is the most dangerous for a potential relapse and should be carefully planned, including physical exercise, outdoor activities, sports, etc. Always avoid bars, game rooms, and other environments where desire for the addiction can be triggered.
- *Spiritual life.* The spiritual component is also fundamental in reintegration. The life of addictions now belongs to the past, and the individual should begin a new life. Guilt, which is common among former addicts, finds forgiveness in a loving Father. And in relation to the future, God promises protection and continuous support.

A wonderful promise from God for those who struggle against addiction is this: "So do not fear, for I am with you; do not be dismayed, for I am your God. I will strengthen you and help you" (Isaiah 41:10).

Codependence

With the intention of rendering help to those who are chemically dependent, some begin a dangerous path: the relationship of mutual dependence. This problem is frequent in the family of the addict. Although with good intentions, the individual (mother, father, or sibling) ends up struggling in the wrong manner for the addict. The individual demonstrates blind love, ceding to the addict's insistent requests. The individual utilizes a large part of his or her time, effort, and emotional energy but ends up being an obstacle toward recovery.

It is fundamental to seek external professional help to put an end to this dangerous collateral effect.

The Twelve Steps

Initially created by Alcoholics Anonymous, these principles are also used successfully by those who want to give up (or have already given up) gambling, overeating, or compulsive sex:

1. We admitted we were powerless over our addiction— that our lives had become unmanageable.
2. We came to believe that a Power greater than ourselves could restore us to sanity.
3. We made a decision to turn our will and our lives over to the care of God as we understood God.
4. We made a searching and fearless moral inventory of ourselves.
5. We admitted to God, to ourselves and to another human being the exact nature of our wrongs.
6. We were entirely ready to have God remove all these defects of character.
7. We humbly asked God to remove our shortcomings.
8. We made a list of all persons we had harmed, and became willing to make amends to them all.
9. We made direct amends to such people wherever possible, except when to do so would injure them or others.
10. We continued to take personal inventory, and when we were wrong promptly admitted it.
11. We sought through prayer and meditation to improve our conscious contact with God as we understood God, praying only for knowledge of God's will for us and the power to carry that out.
12. Having had a spiritual awakening as the result of these steps, we tried to carry this message to other addicts, and to practice these principles in all our affairs.

These support groups have achieved considerable success for decades. The fundamental principles are: trust in God as the main authority and source of power; total sobriety as a goal; commitment to help people who want to abandon their addictions; and confidentiality among participants.

1. "Kids' Top Searches Include 'Porn,'" *BBC News*, August 12, 2009, http://news.bbc.co.uk/2/hi/technology/8197143.stm.

2. "Italian Men Suffer 'Sexual Anorexia' After Internet Porn Use," *Ansa*, March 4, 2011, http://www.ansa.it/web/notizie/rubriche/english/2011/02/24/visualizza_new.html_1583160579.html; "Is Internet Pornography Causing Sexual Dysfunctions? A Review With Clinical Re- ports," *Behavioral Sciences* 6, no. 3 (2016): 17, doi:10.3390/bs6030017; D. Pizzol, A. Bertoldo, and C. Foresta, "Adolescents and Web Porn: A New Era of Sexuality," *International Journal of Adolescent Medicine and Health* 28, no. 2 (May 2016): pp. 169–173, doi:10.1515/ijamh-2015-0003.

3. Albert Mohler, "Hijacking the Brain: How Pornography Works," personal blog, February 1, 2010, http://www.albertmohler.com/2010/02/01/hijacking-the-brain-how-pornography-works.

4. Ibid.

5. William M. Struthers, *Wired for Intimacy: How Pornography Hi- jacks the Male Brain* (Downers Grove, IL: IVP, 2009), p. 76.

6. Ibid., p. 69.

7. G. Richards and A. Smith, "Caffeine Consumption and Self- assessed Stress, Anxiety, and Depression in Secondary School Children," *Journal of Psychopharmacology* 29, no. 12 (December 2015): pp. 1236–1247, doi:10.1177/0269881115612404.

8. Subin Park; Yeeun Lee; Junghyun H. Lee, "Association Between Energy Drink Intake, Sleep, Stress, and Suicidality in Korean Adolescents: Energy Drink Use in Isolation or in Combination With Junk Food Consumption," *Nutrition Journal* 15, no. 1 (October 2016): p. 87; G. S. Trapp et al., "Energy Drink Consumption Is Associated With Anxiety in Australian Young Adult Males," *Depression and Anxiety* 31, no. 5 (May 2014): pp. 420–428, doi:10.1002/da.22175.

9. Mayo Clinic Staff, "Caffeine Content for Coffee, Tea, Soda and More," Mayo Clinic, http://www.mayoclinic.org/healthy-lifestyle/nutrition-and-healthy-eating/in-depth/caffeine/art-20049372, last updated May 30, 2014.

7

The Sentiment of Guilt

Many people live with a burden of guilt. This results in conflicts and the following characteristics: insecurity, perfectionism, constant self-accusation, fear of failure (with the consequent state of permanent vigilance), and being overly demanding of others. A sense of guilt is a useful resource when it stimulates correct and respectful conduct and favorably getting along with others. A real sense of guilt is a symptom of an alert conscience that serves for self-censure and to prevent failures and lack of morals.

For many years, Carlos lived as if he had no guilt regarding the family he had abandoned and the daughter who grew up with a series of emotional problems because of what she experienced in childhood. Now, living in a rest home and sensing death approaching, finally his conscience seemed to wake up. However, what could be done with this feeling? He was no longer able to ask his wife for forgiveness, and his daughter refused to visit him. His despair and frustration increased day after day.

The solution to guilt is found in seeking to make reparation whenever possible, to ask God for forgiveness as well as the people who were offended. Did you know that God is willing to forgive even the greatest mistakes, even those that are unforgivable at the human level? "Though your sins are like scarlet, they shall be white as snow; though they are red as crimson, they shall be like wool" (Isaiah 1:18). To receive forgiveness and reconciliation from God, it is also necessary to forgive others; this helps in the process of forgiving oneself.

Regarding unnecessary or exaggerated guilt, the process requires certain attitudes. Among the main ones we can cite are the following:

- *Do what is right, and rest in God.* Make decisions and form attitudes based on divine principles, and rest in God regarding the results and consequences.
- *Learn lessons from your errors and mistakes.* After asking God for forgiveness and also asking the individuals affected by your mistakes, and seeking to make reparation, make this a learning experience and a motivation to respond in a different manner in the future.
- *Open your heart to someone who is trustworthy.* Talking about your feelings of guilt with a trustworthy friend helps to organize your own ideas. In all cases, it serves as a relief to reduce part of the tension created by this feeling.

When the Conscience Becomes Perverted

The conscience does not always provide a wise standard of conduct. Sometimes the conscience is too narrow and restrictive. In some people the conscience has no limits. Those who have a severe, restrictive conscience expect that others will react in the same manner as they do. And those without limits think all things are good, even what is bad. This is why Proverbs 16:25 states, "There is a way that appears to be right, but in the end it leads to death."

Therefore, it is necessary to count on ethical principles found in the Bible. The apostle Paul warns his disciple Timothy regarding those who, having an insensitive conscience, would order believers to do absurd things (1 Timothy 4:2, 3).

An insensitive conscience is incapable of serving as a guide of trustworthy conduct.

Healthy in the Right Proportion

A study carried out by Grazyna Kochanska and her colleagues verified that the feeling of guilt, in the right amount, helps children to observe rules and respect others. A total of 106 boys and girls from two to five years of age participated in this study. To verify the measure of guilt, the researchers made the children believe that they had ruined a valuable object. Afterward, they observed the behavior of each one, and the opinion of each child's mother was requested. These are the most important results:

- The girls showed greater feelings of guilt than the boys.
- The preschool children from stable families demonstrated less guilt.
- The children with feelings of guilt broke fewer rules than those who did not feel guilt.
- The right proportion of guilt helps to prevent bad behavior.

Forgiveness of the Father

One of the most beautiful and well-known parables Jesus told is that of the prodigal son recorded in Luke 15:11–32. It tells the story of a father and two sons, one of whom grew tired of the calm and peaceful life and decided to abandon everything and look for freedom away from home. As if this rebellious and ungrateful attitude was not bad enough, he also asked for his part of the family inheritance—something customarily received after the father's death. The father, respecting his son's choice, gave him the money. And the son left home.

Free from paternal restrictions, the young man began to squander the money by drinking, partying, and being promiscuous. While his financial resources lasted, he was surrounded by "friends." The money ran out, and he found himself starving. What should he do? He went to find a job and ended up tending pigs, a humiliating task for someone of Jewish origin. The young man who had bragged about his freedom suddenly found himself a slave to his circumstances. The one who had complained about the food at his father's table was now tempted to eat the slop in a pig trough to keep from starving to death. Where were his "friends," the women, the parties?

The text states that the young man had decided to go to "a distant country," an appropriate symbol for sin, since it takes us far from God and from ourselves. It rips away all good things in our life, nurturing for some time the illusion of freedom and joy. But there is no true joy far from God in the "distant country." What the young man discovered is that in the "distant country" there is only frustration, sadness, humiliation, emptiness, and guilt.

In the midst of that deplorable situation, he decided to return home with the intention of being accepted by his father as one of his slaves. This son still had a lot to learn about the man he had turned his back on. However, even though his understanding was limited, he knew that his father was just and loving. It was this thought that made him consider returning. It is always the kindness of God that leads us to repentance and attracts us to Him (Romans 2:4; Jeremiah 31:3).

With his head down, his tattered clothing and a ton of guilt upon his shoulders, the young man walked toward home. His father saw him in the distance, ran to his son, embraced him warmly, and covered his son's misery with his own robe. The father had always been waiting. The father had never stopped loving his son. For this reason, he received the repentant young man as his son, without reminding him of his sins. The past was forgotten; the sins were forgiven; no one could say anything to the contrary.

Satan, the prodigal son who never returned to the Father, is the one who tells the lie that the Lord cannot accept sinners back unless they are good enough to be able to return. If the sinner waits until "good enough" happens, he or she will never return to God.

The main message of this parable is the love of the father, who clearly represents God. He accepts us, forgives us, and loves us always. This knowledge will make a great difference in the life of Carlos and of every sinner who lives under the heavy cloud of a sense of guilt.

Have you made the decision to return to the Father?

Test Yourself

There is an intimate relationship between certain behaviors and guilt. The following questions present behaviors associated with guilt. Answer YES or NO.

1. Did you grow up in an environment where there were authoritarianism and intimidation? _____
2. Is it very difficult to forgive your own mistakes? _____
3. Is it difficult for you to forgive those who offend you?

   _____
4. Are you constantly afraid of breaking some social rule?
5. Are you frightened when faced with the possibility of bad news? _____
6. Do you feel frightened whenever you think about the future? _____
7. Do you become very upset when something does not turn out perfectly? _____

8. Do you feel excessively bothered with a lack of punctuality? _____

9. Do you often feel insecure? _____

10. Do you easily feel upset with yourself and with others? _____

11. Do you become excessively concerned about what other people may think about you? _____

12. In your imagination, is God always upset because of your sins and imperfections? _____

If you answered YES to more than three questions, you are prone to false guilt and should seek solutions. Begin with the counsel in this chapter, and if this is not enough, seek the help of a professional.

8

A Monster
Within

In spite of her age—she was only six years old—when Isabel threw fits, no one wanted to be around her. It was frightening and pitiful. The more she reacted in this way, the more bullying she suffered, resulting in a vicious circle of provocation, explosions of rage, and more provocations. She simply lost control and would attack her classmates and teacher. Most of the time, she was sweet and introspective, which led the teachers and school counselors to suspect that she was expressing some hidden hurt or anger relating to some situation, possibly in her family. Besides, her father had not been to the parent-teacher meetings for quite some time.

Even though she was just a child, Isabel knew that hate, anger, and aggression did not bring her any benefits. However, they are strong tendencies, and many people do not know how to deal with them, whether they are children or adults. As a consequence, people become bitter and pay for this with their own health, in addition to damaging their relationships.

Anger and hate can show up occasionally, and as human feelings, they are not completely avoidable. However, when they surpass the level of being sporadic, they are reactions that cause devastation in family, social, and work relationships. Physical aggression is unacceptable in any human group and should be prevented.

It appeared that Isabel was not suffering from physical aggression, but it was evident that she was suffering some type of lack of love. Something was not right in her home.

How to Avoid Anger and Aggressiveness

By observing oneself and adopting simple habits of calmness and tranquility, one can control the impulses of anger and aggressiveness. Here are some suggestions:

- *Consider the true importance of the situation.* Ask yourself: Is the reason for my anger important? What would happen if things do not turn out my way? Is it worthwhile to expend so much adrenaline? Will I regret this if I lose my composure?
- *Breathe deeply and calm down.* Breathing relaxes us. When you feel anger approaching, breathe slowly and deeply. Give yourself instructions: "Calm down, nothing is going to happen! Control yourself, this will soon go away." It was Thomas Jefferson who originated the famous saying: "When angry, count to ten before you speak. If very angry, count to a hundred." Here's a hint: never send an e-mail when you are angry. If you wish, you can write it but save it as a draft. Read the message again several hours later and reconsider.
- *Try to distract yourself.* Thinking about what caused your anger is simply adding fuel to the fire. Pray to God, asking for help to overcome the negative feeling, and become involved in some activity that occupies your mind with other concerns until the anger has decreased.

- *Choose the right solution.* Avoid saying phrases like these to other people: "You are selfish." "Your attitude is always the same toward me." "You do not care about what I think." Try to express yourself with positive statements: "I would like for you to try to do this in another way." "I am saddened by this attitude." "How can I help you?"

- *Do not consider your opponent as an enemy.* When someone upsets you with their behavior or words, do not think that this individual is provoking you. Think about other reasons and circumstances that explain this behavior. If he or she really has bad intentions, you will see that this individual is an unhappy person and needs compassion.

- *Practice forgiveness.* Forgiving does not mean losing the battle. An old Brazilian proverb states, "Forgive your offender and you will come out the winner." Forgiving not only produces calmness in you but also in the other person, who, additionally, will end up respecting you for your nobleness and generosity.

- *Be grateful.* The Bible states, "Give thanks in all circumstances; for this is God's will for you in Christ Jesus" (1 Thessalonians 5:18). Research confirms that the simple act of showing gratitude for something makes the individual happier. Researchers at the University of California affirm that constantly practicing gratitude can improve health.[1]

- *Pray.* The Bible also says, "Love your enemies and pray for those who persecute you" (Matthew 5:44). Researchers have demonstrated that if a person prays for the individual who upset them, this relieves their bad feeling, dissipating their negative thoughts.[2]

How Anger Affects the Irate Person

Although, in the past, it was considered beneficial to let off steam when someone was angry, today it is clear that the risks surpass any small advantage that could be obtained through these bad attitudes. Compared to people with peaceful habits, those who become angry, in general, face the following situations:

- They have four times more propensity to suffer coronary disease.
- They run greater risks of dying young.
- They experience guilt after explosive attitudes.
- Their relatives and friends avoid them because of their hot temper.
- They have more conflict in their marital relationships.
- They are more prone to using harmful substances (cigarettes, alcohol, other drugs, etc.).
- They run a greater risk of overeating and suffering weight gain.

Before becoming angry, think twice, because it is possible to suppress this conduct and avoid harm.

Annoyed Prophets

The Bible gives some interesting examples of people who allowed themselves to be overcome by anger. Incidentally, this is a unique detail of the Holy Scriptures—its authors did not sugarcoat things, nor did they pose as infallible heroes. Their defects are all recorded there. Do you know why? Because God wants you to know that there is always hope for those who submit to His will and power. Let's talk about two prophets: one from the Old Testament, the other from the New Testament.

Jonah received a difficult mission from God: he was to preach to the people of Nineveh. This city with more than one hundred thousand inhabitants was the capital of the terrible Assyrian Empire. These people were so evil that they were not content with just killing their opponents—they tortured them. They were enemies of Israel, and God wanted His prophet to go to their capital city and take a message. Now, this was just asking too much!

Jonah fled from this mission. He took a ship going in the opposite direction. After being thrown overboard, the prophet was swallowed by a huge fish; three days later, he was regurgitated onto the beach. While in the belly of the fish, Jonah prayed and repented. He went to the Assyrian city, presented the message that it would be destroyed if its inhabitants did not repent, then he turned around and sat down to see what was going to happen. But nothing happened. The Ninevites repented and changed their attitude—the entire city! This made the prophet mad. After all, had he not announced its destruction? He became angry with God's mercy, and he complained to the Creator.

God only asked, "Is it right for you to be angry?" (Jonah 4:4). And God remained silent, letting His son reflect on the matter.

A while later, God returned to speak, revealing a little more of His character of love: "And should I not have concern for the great city of Nineveh, in which there are more than a hundred and twenty thousand people who cannot tell their right hand from their left—and also many animals?" (Jonah 4:11). God is compassionate, forgiving, and patient. He loves all, including the animals! In the book of Jonah, we see the Creator working for the salvation of the people of Nineveh and that of His own angry prophet.

In the New Testament, when transformation is mentioned, one of the personalities who most captures our attention is John, also known as one of the "sons of thunder." Woe to the person who might have crossed his path on a bad day! On one occasion, he asked Jesus for permission to call fire from heaven against certain opponents! But the time spent with the Master molded the character of this disciple. In a few years, he was no longer a "son of thunder," but instead he was known as "the disciple of love." What was the secret? It is very simple: proximity to Jesus. Those who experience this can say, like Paul, "I have been crucified with Christ and I no longer live, but Christ lives in me. The life I now live in the body, I live by faith in the Son of God, who loved me and gave himself for me" (Galatians 2:20).

We do not need to struggle alone. God is the One who is most interested in our inner peace. He offers this blessing to everyone who wants it, even to a six-year-old child like Isabel. Unfortunately, in her home, there was no type of religious practice that could lead her to a relationship with her heavenly Father.

Test Yourself

To learn whether you are prone to anger, answer YES or NO to these questions:

1. Is it difficult for you to forget the bad things others do to you? _____

2. When you are not in agreement with your friends, do you end up in a heated argument? _____

3. When you think of your opponent, do you get stomach pains and a rapid heart rate? _____

4. Do you become upset when you need to wait in line? _____

5. Do you become angry with yourself when you cannot control your emotions? _____

6. Do you become very upset when others are not punctual or do not do things completely? _____

7. Do you have a tendency to not remember anything that you have said while you were furious? _____

8. Have you noticed harmful effects on your relationships because of your bad temper? _____

9. After being upset, do you feel a strong desire to eat, smoke, or drink alcohol to compensate for what has taken place? _____

10. Have you ever become angry to the point of hitting a person or an object? _____

Results:

- If you answered YES to eight or more questions, seek help as soon as possible so you can control your anger. Your personal, family, and work relationships are at serious risk.

- If you answered YES to four to seven questions, this is a warning that your anger is near a dangerous level. Seek to develop patience and tolerance, and you will be able to live in a different way, keeping calm and yielding. Observe others and learn how to get what you want using good manners.

- If you answered YES to three or fewer questions, you are in the right place to face anger and hate. Continue in this manner, because you are a person who is hard to upset.

---

1. Robert A. Emmons and Michael E. McCullough, "Counting Blessings Versus Burdens: An Experimental Investigation of Gratitude and Subjective Well-being in Daily Life," *Journal of Personality and Social Psychology* 84, no. 2 (2003), http://greatergood.berkeley.edu/pdfs/GratitudePDFs/6Emmons-BlessingsBurdens.pdf; Mei-Yee Ng and Wing-Sze Wong, "The Differential Effects of Gratitude and Sleep on Psychological Dis- tress in Patients With Chronic Pain," *Journal of Health Psychology* 18, no. 2 (February 2013): pp. 263–271, doi:10.1177/1359105312439733.
2. Alex M. Wood et al., "Gratitude and Well-being: A Review and Theoretical Integration," *Clinical Psychology Review* 30, no. 7 (November 2010): pp. 890–905, doi:10.1016/j.cpr.2010.03.005.

9

Tips from
the Creator

Imagine as you walked along a beach that you saw "In the beginning, God created the heavens and the earth" written in the sand. As you read the words, a jovial surfer comes along and says, "These words just *appeared* in the sand." Would you believe this explanation? What if he told you that the waves had hit the beach, and the wind had blown against the grains of sand until they were organized in that way? Would you still find this story hard to believe? And if he finally said that all this took place during millions of years? Would that help?

Of course, we are not able to believe a story like this. Intuitively we know that information depends upon a source of information. It does not come out of nowhere. If a phrase written in the sand led us to this conclusion, what can be said of the tremendous amount of information contained in the code of life, our DNA?

The complexity of life points to a project, which points to a Project Designer. This is exactly what Paul wrote in Romans 1:19, 20, "What may be known about God is plain to them, because God has made it plain to them. For since the creation of the world God's invisible qualities—His eternal power and divine nature—have been clearly seen, being understood from what has been made, so that people are without excuse."

God is the Creator of life, and there is no one better than Him to tell us how our body functions in the most appropriate manner. The good news is that He left us an instruction manual within the Holy Bible. Curiously, the eight main tips from the Maker (which some call "natural remedies") are listed at the beginning, in Genesis, the first book of the Scriptures. If we follow them, they can bring physical, mental, and spiritual health.

Look at this chapter as a prescription from the Doctor of all doctors. Seven healthy attitudes have been confirmed by scientific research. You can trust and believe them, because they really work! And best of all, they are free! Begin with the ones you consider the easiest (who knows, maybe drinking more water) and gradually progress into practicing the others. The eighth tip we have left for the last chapter. It is a surprise! You will see the difference that it made in the life of stressed-out Paul, anxiety-ridden Laura, depressed Carlos, and even little Isabel with her temper tantrums. But resist the temptation to flip over to that chapter now. First, read what comes next. Ask God to help you apply these concepts in your life and return to these "prescriptions" as many times as you may need.

First tip: Drink Water[1]

"Now the earth was formless and empty, darkness was over the surface of the deep, and the Spirit of God was hovering over the waters" (Genesis 1:2).

The human body is seventy percent water. Therefore, it is clear that constantly replacing the water that we lose promotes health and longevity. Water cleanses the body and eliminates impurities in the blood. Every hour, ten times the volume of blood in the body passes through the kidneys to be examined and purified.

Not drinking water often leaves the body vulnerable to inflammation and infections, especially in the kidneys and the urinary tract. But what is the ideal amount of water that we should drink every day? On average, eight glasses per day are recommended between meals, avoiding any intake of liquid with food.

- *Benefits of water.* When you do drink enough water, your body feels well and sends a positive signal to the brain. This helps to improve mood and, consequently, productivity.

  When the stomach receives water, the sensation of satiety is prolonged. Additionally, it is good to remember that water does not contain calories, fat, carbohydrates, or sugar!

  Water hydrates the skin, which helps to increase the elasticity and delay the signs of aging.

  Water helps to strengthen the body's defense system. When strengthened, it can better fight against disease.

- *What if I don't drink water?* If you feel tired, one of the reasons could be a lack of water. It eliminates toxins and waste that can harm the body. Besides this, when you only ingest small amounts of water, the heart has to work harder to pump blood.

  Many times, the reason for headaches and migraines has to do with dehydration. When a headache occurs, before taking any type of medication, drink water to hydrate yourself. It is possible that you can resolve the problem this way.

  Bad breath can be a signal of dehydration. Saliva helps the mouth free itself from bacteria and keeps the tongue hydrated.

  As you can see, water is vital for our body. Drink water!

Second Tip: Soak in the Sun's Rays

"And God said, 'Let there be light,' and there was light" (Genesis 1:3).

The sun's rays exercise multiple effects on the human body. They help to fight bacteria and other microbes. This antiseptic action is produced by ultraviolet rays. If the dose of solar radiation that the skin receives is enough, all vital processes will be stimulated by visible light, as well as through infrared and ultraviolet rays, which cannot be seen. Let's understand how they work:

- *On the skin.* The sun's rays dilate the superficial veins, causing a greater flow of blood to the skin, and contribute toward avoiding the accumulation of blood in the internal organs of the thorax and abdomen. They stimulate the production of melanin, a cellular pigment that provides the bronzed tone to the skin, and at the same time strengthen the superficial layers of the skin, protecting against an excess of solar radiation. They have bactericide action, eliminating various harmful microorganisms. Consequently, they help to disinfect and heal superficial wounds.

- *In the bones.* They help to form vitamin D in the skin cells. This vitamin favors the assimilation of calcium ingested in food, contributing decisively in the formation and healthy state of the bones.

- *In the muscles*—The sun's rays improve blood irrigation and stimulate the biochemical energy production processes that occur in the muscle cells. The result is better muscle development and tone, especially beneficial for the sick who are immobilized.

- *In the blood and in the metabolism.* They stimulate hematopoiesis, or the production of red blood cells, white blood cells, and platelets in the bone marrow. They decrease the level of glucose in the blood, thus increasing tolerance to carbohydrates, which is beneficial to diabetics.

- *In the cardiopulmonary system.* The sun's rays stimulate the sympathetic nervous system, elevating blood pressure, pulse, respiration, basal metabolism, and oxygen intake. However, as the skin begins to become tanned and more resistant, blood pressure and basal metabolism decrease, causing the pulse and respiration to become slower.

- *In the nervous system.* They stimulate the nerve endings in the skin, favorably influencing the brain and bringing about a soothing sensation of well-being.
- *In the endocrine system.* The light stimuli that reach the retina are transmitted to the brain in the form of nervous impulses that act, among other organs, in the pituitary gland, controlling the production of hormones in the other endocrine glands. The activation of the ovaries and the testicles, for example, depend in large part on the amount of light that reaches the retina.
- *Caution.* The longer the time spent under solar rays and the lighter the skin, the greater the negative effects will be. These effects include first-degree burns, skin aging, and even skin cancer. In the eyes, too much sun can trigger conjunctivitis (inflammation of the eye) and keratomalacia (inflammation of the cornea), in addition to favoring the formation of cataracts and macular degeneration (alteration of the retina with loss of vision).
- *Directions.* In the morning, open the window in your bedroom and draw back the curtains and blinds. Walk outdoors daily, even when it is cloudy. When possible, between 7:00 and 9:00 a.m. or between 4:00 and 5:00 p.m., take a "sunbath." Approximately twenty to thirty minutes of sun exposure is enough. If the location where you work is totally enclosed, spend some time outdoors during the lunch hour. When doing physical exercise, give preference to being outdoors or in a well-illuminated environment with the windows open.

Third Tip: Breathe Deeply

"So God made the vault [atmosphere]. . . . God called the vault 'sky' " (Genesis 1:7, 8).

The nose is our personal air-conditioning system: it warms cold air, cools hot air, and filters out impurities.

Air contains approximately twenty percent oxygen, with the rest being nitrogen and other gases. Since the human body functions with oxygen, each one of the cells needs to receive a constant and renewed supply of these gases or it will die.

Daily, the lungs process about twelve cubic meters (about 425 cubic feet) of air, which enters into the respiratory tract and hits the pulmonary alveoli, reaching an area greater than seventy square meters. The problem is that the same air that transports vital oxygen can also carry other, less healthy gases and additional particles that reach the alveoli and other regions, where they produce irritation.

Generally, air pollution acts as a coadjutant factor in a person's diseases, because it aggravates the already existing situation. People with respiratory and cardiovascular diseases are the most susceptible to harm from air pollution.

We need to breathe. In spite of air pollution, we need to breathe. It is important to spend as much time as possible in contact with nature and in rural areas, where we can find cleaner air.

When we breathe regularly, calmly, and deeply, besides irrigating the brain, the air reaches all parts of the lungs, allowing the blood to adequately circulate through them. There is also an increase of resistance to infections of the respiratory tract (larynx, the trachea, and the bronchi); the mucus retained in the respiratory tract mobilizes and comes out through expectoration or coughing; resistance to infections increases; intellectual performance improves; and irritability is reduced.

Follow these tips for better breathing:

- Eliminate smoke from closed environments.
- Regularly clean the air ducts and filters in air-conditioners.
- Air out your house, opening doors and windows at least once each day. On cloudy or smog-filled days, do this at night or early in the morning.
- If possible, sleep with an open window to ventilate the room.

- Use air purifiers in moderation.
- Do not leave a car running in a garage adjacent to the house or near an open window.
- Do aerobic physical exercise (run, swim, bike, walk vigorously).
- Maintain your car engine so that it can run efficiently.
- Drink water, at least six to eight glasses per day.
- Keep skin clean and hydrated.
- Wash your hair frequently.
- Dispose of trash or waste material properly.
- When looking for a residence, seek locations with better air quality.
- Make a habit of spending weekends and holidays outside of the city. Breathe the pure country air.
- Do not exercise in locations with heavy automobile traffic.

Fourth Tip: Eat Well

"Then God said, 'I give you every seed-bearing plant on the face of the whole earth and every tree that has fruit with seed in it. They will be yours for food' " (Genesis 1:29).

The cardiologist Everton Padilha Gomes carried out a study entitled Advento-Incor, during his doctorate studies in cardiology at the School of Medicine at São Paulo University (USP). The purpose of the long-term study was to analyze the lifestyle of Seventh-day Adventists and the prevalence of precipitating factors for chronic diseases, especially cardiovascular diseases. The results for those who follow the health principles of the Seventh-day Adventist lifestyle, including vegetarianism, were compared to people who did not follow these principles.

Research in the United States had already demonstrated that people who followed the health recommendations of the Seventh-day Adventist Church, such as a balanced diet and physical exercise, lived up to ten years longer than the average American. Gomes reproduced the North American research study in São Paulo with 1,500 Seventh-day Adventists between the ages of thirty-five and seventy-four.

The participants were divided into three groups: strict vegetarians, lacto-ovo vegetarians (vegetarians who eat eggs and dairy), and people who consume meat. The group of vegetarians obtained the most significant responses: a ten percent reduction in waist measurement and total cholesterol ten percent lower. The rates that indicate a predisposition to diabetes and alterations in the blood vessels were encouraging: a twenty percent reduction.

Gomes draws on the data to reinforce that "the most important thing is to increase the consumption of fruit, vegetables and legumes at meals so that vegetarians eat a balanced diet."

At the beginning of the study, Gomes himself maintained his customary habits until, little by little, he gave in: "Either I would keep up with my self-justification and then suffer the consequences of an inadequate lifestyle, many results of which I was beginning to experience, or I had to yield to the evidence," he confessed.

Fortunately, he opted for the most rewarding route. His dedication to the Advento study provided the challenge he needed. His weight of 282 pounds (128 kilos) and body mass index of 41 began to bother him. Additionally, he wanted his medical "talk" to be in harmony with his own health practices. "I can say that 'I dusted off' many things that I was aware of regarding medicine and many things that I knew through the Adventist Church, which I was not putting into practice," he confirmed.

From the moment of his decision for a new lifestyle, he affirms that no magic formula was necessary, no special diet: "I adopted a regular diet of three daily meals consisting of simple food. I also eliminated sugar and the majority of pre-prepared food."

The hours after work spent reading emails, on social networks, or watching media were substituted by time on the treadmill. "It was not easy, especially during the first month. The astonishing thing is seeing how the body is really dependent on certain things. Initially, I felt like I had no strength. Then it became easier. Currently, without exaggeration, I feel nauseous with the smell of certain foods. My taste has become more refined. Anyway, I feel that my body is functioning better. In three months, my clinical exams changed significantly and positively. Not even with my patients, who make use of more sophisticated medications, did I see some of the changes that I experienced," he emphasizes.

The cardiologist lost almost 110 pounds (50 kilos) in one year. While he applied the study to volunteers, he himself had the greatest benefit. Currently, he feels more freedom to counsel his patients, because they see the difference in his own lifestyle.

Besides the low calories, good proteins, fats, vitamins, and minerals that they contain, foods such as oranges, broccoli, and tomatoes have admirable medicinal qualities. These items, called functional food, can be classified into two groups: foods with immunomodulatory action (they possess phytochemicals capable of activating the immunological system) and food with antioxidant activity (they fight free radicals). The truth is that foods were created to supply the nutritional necessities of living beings. Learning about them and how to use them is synonymous with good health.

The best way to ingest food is in the most natural state possible. The ideal is at least fifty percent of the meal consisting of raw food. Prefer whole foods, which are highly nutritional and rich in fiber and capable of reducing exposure to cancerous agents because of their capacity of regulating the intestinal function.

Highly processed food, animal fat and trans fat, sugar, salt, and refined cereals can cause much damage to health, generating obesity, cancer, diabetes, and decreasing immunological resistance. Cold cuts and sodas are part of a long list that has been proven to harm the body.

It is preferable that three meals per day be consumed, eating well in the morning with a light meal in the evening, several hours before sleeping. Also, it is good to avoid ingesting liquids together with food.

Good nutrition begins with a wise choice of the type of food that will be transformed into nutrients necessary to keep the body in good condition. It is in the intestines that these nutrients are absorbed. A diet rich in fiber promotes the proper functioning of the intestines, which is very important for health.

In the nineteenth century, Ellen White counseled: "After the regular meal is eaten, the stomach should be allowed to rest for five hours. Not a particle of food should be introduced into the stomach till the next meal."[2]

The salivary glands take several hours to recharge their "stock" of salivary amylase. When anything is eaten prior to the habitual meal, the brain commands the gland to liberate saliva. The stomach also needs a "rest" between one meal and another. So seek to eat at regular times and avoid snacking between meals.

Fifth Tip: Exercise

"The Lord God took the man and put him in the Garden of Eden to work it and take care of it" (Genesis 2:15).

One thing is certain, and doctors throughout the whole world agree with this: regular physical exercise provides benefits that no medication can offer. After all, we were created for an active life.

In his book, *Spark: The Revolutionary New Science of Exercise and the Brain*, a professor and psychiatrist from Harvard, John Ratey, affirms that toxic levels of stress wear out the connections between billions of neurons, and chronic depression contracts certain areas of the brain. On the other hand, physical exercise liberates a flow of neurochemicals and growth factors that can reverse this process, helping to support the cerebral infrastructure. This even contributes to the capacity for learning.[3]

There are many other advantages to the practice of physical exercise:

- It helps to strengthen the heart and increases lung capacity, which helps with the efficient completion of common daily tasks.
- Physical exercise helps to prevent osteoporosis, because it helps the bones to retain a greater quantity of calcium.
- Aerobic exercise (running, biking, swimming, and walking at a fast pace) fights stress and depression. In addition to other benefits, it reverses the situation of acquired metabolic diseases (diabetes, cancer, and heart disease).
- It helps to control blood pressure.
- It has been demonstrated that regular physical exercise is capable of reducing high levels of cholesterol and saturated fat in the bloodstream. Besides this, it increases the production of good cholesterol, which protects the arteries.
- Exercising helps one to maintain health, especially if it is accompanied by natural foods. Additionally, the thyroid is stimulated to remain functioning several hours after physical effort, accelerating general metabolism. This helps one to control weight.
- Physical exercise liberates endorphins and causes a sense of well-being; it keeps depression under control; on a long-term basis, it reduces the resting heart rate, and consequently results in less effort from the heart to pump blood; it facilitates

the action of insulin and peripheral circulation, treating Type 2 diabetes; it improves self-image; it reduces the rate of triglycerides; and it favors better sleep. In fact, the list of benefits is even longer than that.

And if you still have not been convinced that you need to exercise, it is important to know that continued inactivity can lead to chronic physical deficiency, making people vulnerable to tiredness and unable to perform physical exertion that may be beyond their normal effort. Sedentariness is a proven cause of various diseases.

So, move! Your body, your brain, and your emotions will thank you.

Sixth Tip: Rest

"By the seventh day God had finished the work he had been doing; so on the seventh day, he rested from all his work. Then God blessed the seventh day and made it holy, because on it he rested from all the work of creating that he had done" (Genesis 2:2, 3).

The idolatry of work has found fertile soil in our inborn disposition for consumption and accumulation of goods. In order to have things, many times we kill ourselves from so much work. Many live at the limits of exhaustion, without taking time to enjoy life. Resting involves more than suspending activities. It is renewal and reconstruction. Let's review some ideas that can help you to have a little more rest.

- *Work the right amount.* Stop your workday at the normal time and go home, leaving all related problems at work. If you think that without you the work cannot go on or the company will fail, remember that you are not indispensable.
- *Relax.* Your muscles need a period of rest and recovery. Remember that one of the best physiological methods of relaxation is physical exercise. A half hour of vigorous walking, for example, is enough.

- *Sleep.* Do not sacrifice your precious hours of sleep in activities that will leave you even more tense. If you have insomnia, avoid taking tranquilizers to sleep. Participate in moderate physical exercise at least four times per week. Do not eat a large amount of food at night. Give preference to food containing fruits and whole-wheat bread. Turn down the lights in the evening. A lukewarm bath before going to bed can also help you to relax. Activities on the computer, such as watching media and news reports, agitate the brain. Instead, read a psalm from the Bible and experience trust in God. Give Him your problems and concerns.

- *One day each week.* Observe one day of the week as a special day of physical, mental, and spiritual rest. As we have already seen, at Creation God concluded the week with a day of rest—the Sabbath. On this day, rest according to the Bible commandment includes the cessation of all common work activities and the designation of time to meditate and carry out activities such as visiting the sick and needy people (Matthew 12:12). If you think that you cannot stop to rest, remember that God created the world in six days and paused on the seventh.

- *Vacation time once a year.* Enjoy your vacation time with your family. This period should be sacred for the family. Go out and do different things, and make a change from your regular activities. Even if you are the owner of your own business, do not miss the chance to set up a plan for vacation. Make arrangements. You need this. Life goes by, children grow up, we grow old and die, and the work remains.

Seventh Tip: Practice Self-Control

"You are free to eat from any tree in the garden; but you must not eat from the tree of the knowledge of good and evil, for when you eat from it you will certainly die" (Genesis 2:16, 17).

113

- Compulsion is the difficulty that a person has to exercise control over a habit. A large number of people struggle against some type of compulsion: binge eating, or addictions such as smoking, drinking, or sex.
- Binge eating is responsible in large part for the high rate of obesity in the world. Many people overeat to fill a void—not just hunger—and they cannot control the impulse through medication.
- Smokers have a greater incidence of cancer of the lungs, mouth, larynx, stomach, pancreas, bladder, and kidneys than nonsmokers. Stomach and duodenal ulcers are sixty percent more common among them. The addiction to smoking removes calcium from the bones, accelerating the process of osteoporosis.
- The habit of ingesting alcoholic beverages also has a high price. Alcohol promotes an increase in blood pressure, and it is toxic for the cardiac muscle tissue. It increases the risk of stroke and sudden death resulting from arrhythmias and diseased cardiac muscles, besides contributing to the development of cirrhosis and cancer.
- Resistance to a compulsion begins with exercising self-control, which can be defined in one word: temperance. This is abstinence from all that is harmful and the balanced use of all that is good.
- Keeping yourself informed regarding the importance of a healthy lifestyle helps a great deal, but seeking strength from God also is very important. The strength received through prayer and communion with the Creator will influence our capacity to make changes, substitutions, and shifts in our habits.
- Putting into practice the tips in this chapter would benefit Paul, Laura, Carlos, and even little Isabel. What do you think? If they could be valuable for them, they will also be beneficial for you. Why not begin putting these tips into practice today?

1. Most of this chapter (the tips section) is an adaptation, with permission from the author, Francisco Lemos, of the article, "Os Mais Simples Remédios" ["The Most Simple Remedies"], *Vida e Saúde* [*Life and Health*], July 2014, pp. 9–25.

2. Ellen G. White, *Counsels on Diet and Foods* (Washington, DC: Review and Herald®, 1976), chap. 9, p. 179.

3. John Ratey, *Spark: The Revolutionary New Science of Exercise and the Brain* (New York: Little, Brown, 2008), pp. 13, 14.

10

The Power of Hope

In this chapter, we will focus on the eighth tip from the Maker: trust in God and hope. Will this remedy really work? Can religion really do any good in the life of those who practice it?

Religious involvement reduces psychological stress, which decreases inflammation and the rate of telomere shortening in the cells. Telomeres are like a biological clock for the cell. They shorten during each cell division, and when they disappear, the cells die, causing degeneration of the organ. This explains why religious-minded people live an average of seven to fourteen years longer.

Therefore, religion is only beneficial if it is practiced and is centered on a good relationship with God and with one's fellow human beings. This leads us to remember James 1:27: "Religion that God our Father accepts as pure and faultless is this: to look after orphans and widows in their distress and to keep oneself from being polluted by the world."

True religion is practical and makes us better people here and now. At the same time, it points to a future of hope. Hope is the main emotion in relation to the future. This quality, together with optimism and the ability to maintain good relationships, make up the best prevention against mental illnesses.

Hope offers a resistance to shock. When a natural disaster or a personal misfortune occurs, those who firmly believe that a solution exists will experience an additional measure of strength to recover from material losses and their own setback. As the psychologist Viktor Frankl explains, almost all of the survivors of the Nazi concentration camps lived through the experience because they maintained their hope of freedom until the end, because they did not accept the idea that this situation was the end of their existence, and they concentrated on the hope of being liberated some day from that infernal situation.

To Increase Hope

If hope is such an important condition and affects so many areas of our present and future, we should learn ways to promote it. Note this list of tips to help you to strengthen and develop hope:

- *Develop thoughts filled with hope.* When you look to the future, make an effort to think positively. What you expect at the beginning determines the final outcome of things. When you go through a positive experience, reflect on the positive qualities that made it possible.
- *Reject negative thoughts.* Many pessimistic thoughts contain mistakes of logic that we have to learn to fight. If your vacations were not good in the past, you cannot conclude that in the future they will always be unpleasant. You should look for specific factors that can be changed with the purpose of gaining control over past failures and instilling hope for the future.
- *Think about the past calmly.* Look back on past events without anxiety. Especially, concentrate on pleasant things and demonstrate gratitude and appreciation for your life

experience. When you do this, you will see the future in a happier and more positive light, because there are enough blessings in your past to look to the future with hope.

- *Change your routine.* When despair oppresses you, change your routine in some aspect. Visit a new environment and distract yourself with something different. Invite a friend you have not seen for many years to talk. Listen to new music. And if you do not observe the Sabbath, how about trying that out now? These variations will renew your spirit to the point where you can look to the future with hope.

- *Cultivate optimism.* Hope and optimism are intimately connected. There are always two ways of interpreting the same fact. For example: (1) "What if this headache is caused by a tumor?" or (2) "This headache will pass." In the absence of a precise diagnosis, it is better to opt for the second way of thinking. Everything has a positive and negative side. Consider both sides, evaluate the situation, and gather all information available. Then, feel satisfied with the positive side and enjoy the results.

- *Read and meditate.* Always have good books as companions—books that present subjects of a high standard and with the most profound knowledge possible. Think on the ideas in these books, and you will find strength to reinvigorate your hope. The Gospels, Psalms, and Proverbs contain inspired texts that have served as support and have strengthened the hope of many people.

- *Find a good social circle.* Hope is strengthened with the presence of hopeful and positive people. Seek to be in the company of those who have hope, and befriend these people. Spend your time in the company of good people.

- *Transmit encouragement and hope to others.* Part of your personal growth consists in reflecting to others your own positive influence. When speaking to someone who is going through a difficult situation, encourage them and help them to flee from despair. Direct their attention to other pleasant or neutral subjects until the storm has passed.

- *Care for your physical well-being.* Keep yourself in shape with good health and satisfaction; both are conditions that help you to look toward the future with hope. Take care of your health consciously so that your thoughts are filled with hope. Put into practice the tips that you have learned in the previous chapter.

Religious Hope

In addition to being a positive attitude for the future and a source of good mental health, hope is a quality that is intimately related to religious faith. The majority of religions are founded on hope, or count on a strong component of faith. For the believer, hope is a gift from God that relates the past to the present and the future, for reaching a happy and definitive end.

Note the most outstanding characteristics of hope in the religious context:

- *It refers to the hope of salvation.* Religious hope provides the ultimate solution to the problem of suffering. Eternal salvation is reached according to the plan created by God Himself: "The hope of eternal life, which God, who does not lie, promised before the beginning of time" (Titus 1:2).
- *It is essential for survival.* In a world filled with injustice and suffering, we need to find refuge in the word of the psalmist, who offers hope in God as a means of vital support: "I remain confident of this: I will see the goodness of the Lord in the land of the living. Wait for the Lord; be strong and take heart and wait for the Lord" (Psalm 27:13, 14).

- *Obtaining it requires more than human effort.* In the biblical context, it is not only personal interest and decision but divine intervention that makes possible the great gift of hope. The apostle Paul affirmed that true hope comes freely from God: "Our Lord Jesus Christ himself and God our Father, who loved us and by his grace gave us eternal encouragement and good hope" (2 Thessalonians 2:16).

- *It provides joy.* True hope is a reason for joy, happiness, and well-being. Paul makes use of this idea in a very clear manner: "Be joyful in hope, patient in affliction, faithful in prayer" (Romans 12:12). "May the God of hope fill you with all joy and peace as you trust in him, so that you may overflow with hope by the power of the Holy Spirit" (Romans 15:13).

- *It remains until Jesus returns.* Hope, according to the Bible, will culminate with the return of Christ to this world, a fact that indicates the end of fear, injustice, and suffering: "We wait for the blessed hope: the appearing of the glory of our great God and Savior, Jesus Christ" (Titus 2:13).

- *It includes the certainty of resurrection.* Christian hope encourages the believer by assuring them that one day they will be resurrected for eternal salvation: "Brothers and sisters, we do not want you to be uninformed about those who sleep in death, so that you do not grieve like the rest of mankind, who have no hope. . . . For the Lord himself will come down from heaven, with a loud command, with the voice of the archangel and with the trumpet call of God, and the dead in Christ will rise first" (1 Thessalonians 4:13, 16).

- *It is centered in a perfect and eternal reward.* "Praise be to the God and Father of our Lord Jesus Christ! In his great mercy, he has given us new birth into a living hope through the resurrection of Jesus Christ from the dead, and into an inheritance that can never perish, spoil or fade. This inheritance is kept in heaven for you" (1 Peter 1:3, 4).

If religious hope is still not part of your life, try this—study and accept the promises of salvation and eternal life. This acceptance will provide changes that will offer more purpose to your life and a much more complete hope.

Restoration

The incontestable fact is that the past cannot be changed. We have indicated this throughout this book. The future still does not belong to us. What remains, therefore, is the present and what we do with it.

When Laura decided to study the Bible and learn about God, her study activated a chain reaction that she could not have imagined. Laura's decision could not change the past, but it would help to write a future of hope for her and for others.

As she progressed through her Bible studies and deepened her communion with Jesus, she began to feel a discomfort in relation to her father. This time, something was different. Before when she thought about him, she felt hate and contempt. How could he have been insensitive to the point of abandoning his little daughter just so he could "enjoy life"? How could he have been so selfish and not consider that this would leave profound marks on her life? If he had not abandoned the family, perhaps Laura's mother would still be alive. The frightened little girl would not have been raised by a distant aunt, and she would not have immersed herself in books and in her career as a way to suffocate the clamors of her soul. She would not have become such an obstinate, anxious, and intolerant person with the people who surrounded her at work—the only place where she still had some type of social interaction. If her father had not left her home, certainly she would not have developed an aversion to men and today could have a family of her own, a husband, and maybe even children.

Laura could not change any of this, but there was something she could do: forgive her father and reconcile herself with her past. Months prior to discovering what she was learning, this would have been impossible, but now things were different. *She* was different. Hadn't the father of the prodigal son received his son back again? What about "prodigal parents" then? Did they deserve forgiveness too? She had to do this—for herself and for him. This would be the first miracle in this chain reaction.

When she opened the door of the nursing home and stepped inside, Laura felt a cold chill creep up her spine. Her heart beat faster, and her hands began to perspire. Would she have the strength to do this? It had been many years since the last time she had attempted to enter this place—although at that time she had been unsuccessful.

Slowly, she stepped into a room and walked up to a white-haired man, slumped over in a wheelchair, looking aimlessly through the window. His back was facing her, and he did not notice her approaching. Laura noticed how thin he was, how his skin seemed to hang on his bones because of the advancing cancer. He was only a shadow of what he had been.

Laura offered a silent prayer, gathered all of her strength and, almost in a whisper, timidly said, "Dad."

That word, that voice . . . How long had it been since he had heard it? Carlos struggled to turn the wheelchair around and look directly into the eyes of the woman in front of him.

"Child? Is it really you? You have come?"

Tears began to stream from their eyes at the same time. "You are not going to believe this! At this exact moment, I was looking to heaven and I thought: 'God, if you exist, give me proof of this. Please, bring my daughter here before I die. I need to ask her to forgive me, I need to . . .' "

His voice quivered. The man who had once been known as Big Carlos now was like a defenseless child. The "prodigal parent" was humiliated, ragged, destroyed. He had squandered everything and had lost what was most precious.

What would my heavenly Father do in my place? Laura thought. And she waited no longer. Quickly closing the distance that separated them, she warmly embraced her father, lingering as tears flowed down her cheeks.

"Dad, God exists, and He just answered your prayer. I forgive you."

The second miracle.

When Laura arrived at work on Monday morning, everyone noticed that something was different. To begin with, she arrived at the office smiling and greeted everyone with a "Good morning." Then she began to call her employees one by one into her office.

"Have a seat, Paul. Is everything OK with you?"

Paul seated himself slowly in the chair in front of Laura's desk, evaluating each expression on her face. *Is she sick? Has she gone totally crazy?* he wondered.

"I know that you and everyone else must be thinking that this is all strange. So I decided to talk to each one individually. Not as your supervisor, but as a fellow human being."

Paul sat in silence, almost without blinking.

"First of all, I need to ask for your forgiveness. In the past several months, because of my anxiety and focusing only on the company's success, I ended up mistreating and overloading all of you. I think that I made your life a living hell."

Paul struggled not to nod his head in agreement.

"But something wonderful has happened in my life that has completely changed my perspective. It is going to seem strange, but it is a simple truth. I cannot say that it was anything else:

I had a personal encounter with Jesus. He forgave me, helped me to forgive my father, and allowed me to look toward the future with hope."

Laura picked up her Bible with both hands and continued: "It was by studying this book that I adjusted my focus, and this helped me to see that I could become a different person. People are infinitely more important than things and numbers."

Looking directly into the eyes of her employee, she asked, "Paul, can you forgive me? Please forgive me for all the stress that I caused you. Certainly this must have affected your health and your family, right? Can you forgive me?"

Swallowing hard, he answered hesitantly, "Yes, Laura, I can. I forgive you."

Laura got up, thanked Paul, and concluded, "I promise that from now on everything will be different."

The third miracle.

Paul left his supervisor's office still not understanding exactly what had happened, but he felt better. He felt relieved. It was almost time to go home. Back at his desk, he grabbed a sheet of paper and began to jot down a few words. Then he slipped the sheet into an envelope, placed it into the pocket of his suit jacket, and went home.

"Hi, dear! You look really beautiful today!" he said, hugging his wife tightly—something he had not done for a long time. Kneeling in front of his son, he said, "Put on your shorts. In a little bit we're going to play ball in the backyard."

Looking at his little daughter, he coaxed her, "Come here, sweetie. I have something for you."

Paul took out an envelope from his jacket and gave it to Isabel. Imagining that it might be another letter from the school telling about her tantrums, she opened it with caution. Inside, there was a sheet of paper with the words: "I love you, sweetie."

With her eyes filled with tears, she clung to her father's neck, as he firmly but softly stated to his family, "We are in need of God in this house. We are in need of love."

The fourth miracle.